W9-DGZ-924

DATE DUE

THE DAWN OF THE MIDDLE AGES

IS VOLUME

75

OF THE

Twentieth Century Encyclopedia of Catholicism

UNDER SECTION

VII

THE HISTORY OF THE CHURCH

IT IS ALSO THE

50TH

VOLUME IN ORDER OF PUBLICATION

Edited by HENRI DANIEL-ROPS of the Académie Française

THE DAWN OF
THE MIDDLE AGES

By JEAN-RÉMY PALANQUE

Translated from the French by DOM FINBARR MURPHY

HAWTHORN BOOKS · PUBLISHERS · *New York*

First Edition, September, 1960

NIHIL OBSTAT

Joannes M. T. Barton, S.T.D., L.S.S.

Censor Deputatus

IMPRIMATUR

E. Morrogh Bernard

Vicarius Generalis

Westmonasterii, die XVI JULII MCMLX

CONTENTS

INTRODUCTION

CONSTANTINE

The name of the first Christian emperor marks the beginning of this new era. Constantine's conversion was a decisive turning point. The imperial authority, whose recognition of the Church of Christ had hitherto only taken the form of persecution, now granted her not only peace and liberty but also notable favours and perquisites which were soon to acquire the character of privileges; at a time when Rome's sway extended over almost all the civilized world and when subjects readily adopted the religion of their sovereign, this turn of events was bound to involve sooner or later the transition of the ancient world to Christianity. Naturally such a transition was not accomplished overnight, but very soon, even if conversions were still deficient in numbers and depth, at least the official character accorded to the Church, the spread of ecclesiastical buildings throughout the Empire, and the penetration of the institutions and conduct of society by the principles of the Gospel—these justify use of the term "Christianized" Empire. The whole Empire, then, provides the setting for our study of the various aspects of Church history: relations with the State, organization of the clergy, doctrinal controversies, and Christian life in all its forms. After its primitive age of heroism, Christianity now took on a new form which for several centuries in the East was hardly to undergo alteration, for in its Greek-speaking territories the "Roman" Empire survived without serious mishap right through the Middle Ages: no break of continuity was involved in its becoming the "Byzantine" Empire whose Church in the eleventh century was to secede from the Christian communities of the West. By that time, however, the latter had not been part of the Empire for several centuries: their fortunes merit separate study.

THE BARBARIAN WILDERNESS

No other expression so well describes the state of the West between the fifth and eighth centuries. Scarcely a century after Constantine, Roman supremacy was overthrown, and gradually the Empire was replaced by a host of Germanic kingdoms, often unstable. The society, economy and the civilization of the late Empire long survived without radical changes, but a general impoverishment, a decline of culture, made itself felt; though the rulers of these new states might regard the Roman system with admiration and respect (which did not always happen), they had lost the art of maintaining the political organization, of keeping order in the outlying provinces and in the intellectual atmosphere. This period, which in France is called the Merovingian age (corresponding in the neighbouring countries to the Anglo-Saxon, Visigothic, Vandal and Lombard ascendancies), was a period of decadence for Christianity and secular civilization alike. As for the territories lying to the east and south of the Mediterranean, the tale is not of decadence but of disaster: here in the seventh century victorious Islam swept all before it, wiping out the Christian Churches of Syria, Egypt and North Africa, and for a brief moment even threatening those of western Europe.

CHARLEMAGNE

Like a spell, his name conjures up the renaissance which the West experienced in the eighth and ninth centuries, after the barbarian devastations. The foundation by this Frankish prince of an Empire which was centred on Gaul and confronted that of Byzantium meant the revival of the claim by a state to universal dominion; the civilization which he steadily promoted, spreading it in the wake of his armies from Spain to Germany and Italy, was characterized by a return to Antiquity: the Christianity to which both Empire and civilization aspired was the Christianity of Constantine's Empire and the last epoch of Roman civilization. The Carolingian era accordingly represents an outstanding yet short-lived episode in the history of the Church.

PART I

IMPERIAL CHRISTIANITY

CHAPTER I

STATE RELIGION AND CAESAROPAPISM

Among the problems which arise in a history of the Church of Christ, that of Church-State relations (to which a volume of this series is devoted) is doubtless not the most important, nor one which ought to engage the special attention of a religious inquirer. Yet there are times when this problem takes on a particular importance, when it seems to colour all others. Thus at the beginning of the fourth century the life of the Church was for some years paralysed by imperial persecution, and the authorities of the day made every effort to secure her destruction. Soon afterwards, the political aspects of Church history come to the forefront with a return to toleration, followed by Constantine's conversion. Without neglecting other aspects, which relate to the interior life of the Church, we must first of all examine the attitude of the Roman state towards victorious Christianity.

CONSTANTINE'S CONVERSION

For us the importance of Constantine's conversion lies not in its depth, its quality or even its sincerity (this problem of conscience, which has been the subject of so much writing and discussion, is probably insoluble), but rather in its practical result, which was the conferring of official favour on the ministers of the Church and on the tenets of Christianity. After 313 every Christian community recovered its churches (those at least which had not been destroyed) and the goods belonging to them (even if

they had been confiscated) by virtue of a decree which was circu-
larized to the provincial governors of Africa and the East and
which is often called the Edict of Milan. At the same time the
bishops who were the heads of these communities were granted
considerable subsidies for the erection or embellishment of new
churches. At Rome by the side of the Lateran palace, which
henceforth was to be the residence of the Christian pontiff, the
Lateran basilica was built, and shortly afterwards the Vatican
basilica was erected over the tomb of St Peter; in the East, after
Constantine's triumphal entry in 324, the Holy Places of Palestine were adorned with splendid basilicas on Calvary and
at Bethlehem, and Constantinople saw buildings dedicated
to Peace, to the Apostles, and later to Wisdom (*Sancta
Sophia*).

These favours were extended not only to public buildings but
also to the members of the clergy. Bishops were now recognized
as the heads of the local Churches and entitled on their behalf to
receive gifts and legacies and to administer ever increasing
amounts of property; they were exempted from the taxes and
dues with which citizens were burdened, and given authority to
wield civil jurisdiction over their clerics and even over those of
the laity who should accept or request their judgements, such
judgements being henceforth final and effective. All these privileges, reinforced at the end of the fourth century by the exemption of clerics from curial taxes, recognition of rights of sanctuary
in churches and extension of episcopal jurisdiction, were to be
solemnly confirmed by legislation of the emperor Honorius in
395 and 397. Finally, the principles of the Gospel now won recognition: out of regard for virginity Constantine repealed the
laws hostile to celibacy, and he was severe in his punishment of
crimes and vices contrary to the virtue of chastity, as also of acts
which offended charity: he even declared Sunday a holiday, thus
making incumbent upon all the weekly day of rest in its Christian
form.

THE END OF PAGANISM

Paganism was traditionally bound up with the Roman state,

and it would be an exaggeration to say that the first Christian emperor made any real break with it. Like all his successors until the time of Gratian, Constantine continued to be *pontifex maximus*, and if in certain official documents he denounced the "falsehoods of superstition" or "errors of the pagans", the actual measures effectively taken in his reign were aimed only at certain immoral cults from Syria, sorcery and divination (which were considered politically dangerous) and certain neo-Platonic doctrines. Paganism was purged, but not persecuted. Under Constantine's sons there was a semblance of a more drastic policy, for a law of Constans in 341 (renewed by his brother Constantius II in 353 and 356) decreed the end of "superstition" and the abolition of sacrifices, but this legislation never seems to have been really enforced: even at Rome paganism was still in all its vigour when Constantius visited the Eternal City in 357.

Tolerated hitherto only in practice, paganism found itself once again enjoying protection and patronage during the brief reign (361–363) of Constantine's nephew the emperor Julian, known as the "Apostate": brought up as a Christian, he had been genuinely converted to a rather muddled philosophy, made up of neo-Platonism and mystical polytheism. Julian reopened the temples and attempted to reform the old religion by giving it a structure modelled on that of the Christian Church; while his main efforts were devoted to plaguing the Christians, whom he excluded from the civil service and even from teaching, always he stopped short of making martyrs—for he prided himself on his tolerance. Though the decline of the traditional religion now appeared inevitable, it was temporarily checked by this pagan reaction, in spite of its brief duration: the succeeding emperors Valentinian and Valens tolerated the diverse forms of paganism with the exception of sorcery, astrology and the nocturnal sacrifices already outlawed by Constantine, and the most prominent intellectuals at Rome or in the East remained faithful to the various cults of the past.

After 380 a new era opened under the influence of Ambrose, bishop of Milan. Gratian appears to have relinquished the title of *pontifex maximus* after 379 and his colleague Theodosius, installed in the same year, never assumed it at all: this vital link between paganism and the person of the emperor was now broken. Further separation of the State from the traditional religion was accomplished in 382 by Gratian's legislation for the city of Rome, decreeing the removal of the altar of Victory placed in the hall of the Senate, abolition of the subsidies and immunities enjoyed by the colleges of priests and vestals, and confiscation of their property. The Senate protested against these measures and on four or five occasions appealed to succeeding emperors for the restoration of the altar of Victory—but without success. Another pagan reaction set in with the accession of the usurper Eugenius in 393, but it collapsed in the following year with his defeat at the hands of Theodosius who now put into effect throughout the Empire the laws he had promulgated in 391 and 392. These finally proclaimed a general outlawry of pagan cults, under pain of fines and forfeiture of property. There was no question of the persecution of individuals (pagans were to survive at least until the sixth century) but all external manifestation of the old religion was now forbidden: the temples were closed, destroyed or turned into churches, and the priests were deprived of their privileges. Under Arcadius and Honorius, the sons of Theodosius, new laws repeated these measures which were designed to root out "abominable superstition".

UNION OF CHURCH AND STATE

The removal of Christianity's rival from the field coincided with the first appearance of a thoroughgoing "State religion". Religion was the underlying foundation essential to the ancient city-state, and now that paganism had been rejected men looked to some new official religion which would take its place. Disregarding the Gospel teaching, which enjoined the separation of Caesar's realm from that of God, the Christian emperors carried on the secular traditions of a close partnership between State authority and the powers of religion: like the Pharaohs or the legendary kings of Rome, the Hellenistic monarchs or the Caesars of the Western Empire, Constantine and his successors regarded themselves as representatives of the divinity or as possessed of a divine power and consequently entrusted with authority over the Church as over every other religious body. As early as 314 Constantine summoned a council in an endeavour to settle an ecclesiastical schism in Africa, and in 325 at Nicaea in Bithynia he assembled bishops from every part of the Roman world for what was the first "ecumenical" or universal council: after that, the majority of the councils were held on the initiative of the emperors, who promoted and facilitated their meeting even if they did not lay down the decisions to be taken. At the extreme, the emperor would usurp the position of the rightful leaders of the Church.

This tendency, known as "Caesaropapism", made its first appearance under Constantine's son Constantius II, who imposed his fluctuating dogmatic inclinations on the whole episcopate: between 353 and 360 he inflicted on the Church a genuine reign of terror, banishing those who would not comply, and capriciously determining doctrine in a series of contradictory councils. Yet, though the prelates of the time might rebuke the emperor for heresy or complain of his vagaries, it is noteworthy that they never questioned his right of interfering in this way with religious affairs. The first to rise up in protest against the claims of Caesaropapism seems to have been Ambrose of Milan. "The things of God are not subject to imperial power"; "palaces are the emperor's concern, but churches are the bishop's": with telling phrases he championed the Church's right to liberty. He also maintained that the emperor was not above the Church but part of it, and consequently that the civil authorities should not tolerate the existence of heretical worship or the encroachments of Judaism: his conflict with Valentinian II in 386 and the Callinicum incident in 388 provide illustrations of these uncompromising convictions. In the same way St Augustine was to call upon the assistance of the "secular arm" in order to root out the Donatist schism in Africa (where Constantine and his sons had already set a precedent for such assistance). The trend of the age was totalitarian: only this can explain the fact that those who asserted the Church's right to freedom of action were the first to invoke State intervention against her enemies both inside and outside the fold.

Enemies outside the fold were the instigators of heresy, Jewish proselytizers, apologists of paganism—all of them "slaves of the devil", teachers of falsehood. Within the fold were those Christians who rebelled against priestly authority, and such cases had to be referred to a regular synod or to the judgement of the pope. The Emperor Gratian in 378 and Valentinian III in 445 gave orders to their officials that if any bishops in their respective provinces were summoned before a conciliar assembly or the Roman curia, they were to be despatched under military escort. Thus did the State become a "secular arm" of the Church, as Ambrose and Augustine had desired.

Besides being liable to ecclesiastical authority, however, the emperor was also God's subject and as such bound like all men to the moral law. Ambrose had the courage to remind Theodosius of this fact on a memorable occasion in 390 when the emperor had caused thousands of innocent people to be massacred as a reprisal for a popular rising at Thessalonica: he treated him as a public sinner, delivered a kind of excommunication against him, and imposed a penance followed by a formal absolution. This exercise of authority by a bishop over an emperor on a moral issue, which foreshadows the medieval excommunication of adulterous kings, is testimony of a noble and uncompromising spirit on the part of the Church.

However, such an outcome remained the exception in the Byzantine Empire. Some months after the victory of the bishop of Milan, the western capital, a grievous fate befell the bishop of the eastern capital, St John Chrysostom, after he had defied the Court of Constantinople. It was a complex affair, involving the orthodoxy of Origenism and the jurisdiction of the patriarch over the provinces of Asia, but behind the pretexts which afforded opportunities for settling private scores, the ultimate reason for the patriarch's downfall was the enmity of the Court: the Empress Eudoxia would not endure the fiery bishop's attacks on worldliness and frivolity, and she saw a personal reference in the denunciations he preached against Jezebel or Herodias. Twice exiled, he was deported on the second occasion to Armenia, where he died, and many bishops, clerics, or lay-people believed to be of his "party" were struck down in their turn. It was a dangerous thing to offend the susceptibilities of the imperial court. As a result, churchmen ceased to exert a salutary influence over the rulers of the State and more often retired to a devotional ivory tower: this was especially the case in the East, where in general the prelates were servile and the emperors authoritarian, and where the advent of Justinian was to see caesaropapism established supreme and unimpeded.

BYZANTINE CAESAROPAPISM

As early as the reign of Theodosius II in the sixth century the Court had determined theological disputes at the two councils of Ephesus: the ecumenical assembly of 431, and the so-called "Robber Council" of 449. When the next emperor, Marcian, summoned an ecumenical council at Chalcedon in 451 he left the Church full liberty, but under Zeno and Anastasius ecclesiastical affairs once more came under imperial management: the "Henoticon" or "Edict of Union" which Zeno addressed to the bishops in 484 defined the faith according to the formulas of Nicaea and Ephesus but deliberately omitted those of Chalcedon. In this way the Eastern Empire set itself at odds with those Churches which remained faithful to the conciliar definitions—that is, with the whole of the West—and the ensuing schism lasted more than thirty years. In 518 the Emperor Justin restored orthodoxy, but he did not abandon his claim to dictate dogma, so that the peace and unity of the Church were at the mercy of the emperor's whim. The same tendency soon became apparent under Justinian. At first an active defender of the Catholic faith, respectful of defined dogmas and ready to extend the privileges of the clergy (in judicial matters, for example), Justinian nevertheless considered himself entitled to intervene constantly in Church affairs: besides enforcing ecclesiastical canons by official decrees he even went so far as to complete or to alter them as he thought fit; not only episcopal elections but even clerical or monastic discipline is regulated in his legislation, which enters at times into the most minute detail. Like the Austrian emperor Joseph II he might well be called the "sacristan-king". More serious still was his similar interference in doctrinal disputes. He condemned by official decree the "heresy" of Origen, a third-century exegete, in 543, and the "Three Chapters" of some fifth-century theologians in 544, and on the eve of his death in 565 he even claimed the right to enforce—also by edict—a theory which was patently heterodox. The intervening years had seen him assembling and conducting the fifth ecumenical council in 551, making and un-making patriarchs at Constantinople and popes at Rome, for ever advancing ill-considered proposals in his search for an impossible reconciliation with the Monophysites, and acting on all occasions as if he were the rightful head of the universal Church.

Caesaropapism was now at its zenith, an established tradition which was to remain as long as the Empire lasted. Rather than weary the reader by enumerating all its manifestations throughout the course of Byzantine history, we can confine ourselves to a few examples which will show how the successors of Constantine and Justinian remained faithful to the policy of their great predecessors. Justin II first decided on an edict of union advantageous to the Monophysites (567), but when the latter proved intransigent he changed to a decree enforcing Catholic orthodoxy (571). Heraclius, confronted by new Christological controversies, thought he would put an end to disagreement by banning the various formulas under dispute, but his edict issued in 638, the Ecthesis, only added a new formula, inaugurating yet another heresy. Constans II, still pursuing the never-ending quest for unity, issued in his turn a solemn edict, the Typos of 648, which forbade all controversy.

In the East the bishops nearly always bowed obediently before these official directions, but in Italy (then under Byzantine rule) the Roman pontiff offered resistance on several occasions. Under Justinian, Pope Vigilius had suffered violent treatment from the emperor, who compelled him to come to the East and to sign questionable statements under duress. When in the reign of Heraclius Popes Severinus and John IV condemned the Ecthesis, no conflict ensued since the emperor's attention was engaged elsewhere with the Arab invasion. Under Constans II in 653, Pope Martin I, having secured the condemnation at a Roman council of the Ecthesis and Typos, was seized by Byzantine soldiers, held in confinement on an island of the Cyclades, imprisoned at Constantinople and finally, after an ignominious degradation, deported to the Crimea where he died in wretched circumstances. So too Maximus the Confessor, the monk who led the opposition against the caesaropapism of Constans II, was arrested at Rome and deported to Thrace, thence to the Caucasus, where he died in 662. Finally, the founder of the new Isaurian dynasty, Leo III, also claimed the right to legislate on religious matters, and in 725 his edict decreeing the destruction of images in all churches marked the beginning of the Iconoclastic dispute, a controversy which throughout the eighth century set the emperors against popes and patriarchs, and which provides an outstanding example of imperial interference in the affairs of the Church.

After Constantine's hesitancy and the submissiveness of emperors like Gratian and Theodosius, imperial Christianity at last took its definitive character from the aggressive authoritarianism which from the fifth century onwards was typical of the Byzantine *basileis*. The emperor (as one of them, Justinian II, declared in 687) now regarded himself as "by divine mercy appointed guardian of the faith"—a claim which altogether nullified the independence of the Church. Thus, while the Empire had become Christian, the Church was now controlled by, and completely subject to, the State: for both this situation was equally unfortunate.

CHAPTER II

ECCLESIASTICAL

ORGANIZATION

As it became penetrated by Christianity, the Roman Empire left its mark on the Church not only in the form of the authority which its rulers abused but also in the very structure of its material life and organization. From the first centuries the centres of the Christian community had been those same "cities" which from one end of the Empire to the other were the nuclei of "political" life. Just as the magistrates of each city were formerly elected by all the members of the civic body, so too each Church had a bishop elected by the whole body of faithful in the district. As the number of Christians grew, so bishoprics were founded in most of the cities and in some places (e.g. Latin Africa and Egypt) even in simple townships, so that from the beginning of the sixth century the map of ecclesiastical organization coincided exactly with that of the civil organization: the rule was to have one bishop in each city, enjoying sovereign power within his territory to state doctrine, to ordain and judge his clerics, and to administer the property of the Church. Any interference by one bishop in the province of another and translations from one see to another were condemned by the canons of Nicaea in 325 (confirmed by many later councils). Thus bound for life to the community of the faithful, it was the bishop, rather than magistrates without prestige or officials without authority, who in troubled times became the accredited representative of the people in dealing with public authorities of the barbarian invader.

THE PROVINCES

Above the city, the next administrative division was the province. The bishop of the provincial capital, with his seat next to that of the governor, who was the emperor's representative, considered himself as having a certain authority over his colleagues in the province. The Council of Nicaea officially recognized this principle when it decided that elections and episcopal assemblies should be held according to provinces, presided over by the bishop of the provincial capital, the metropolitan. It fell to the metropolitan, with two other prelates, to consecrate the newly elected bishop, and he was also to assemble his suffragans twice a year (it was laid down) in order to judge appeals from the several episcopal courts or to discuss matters affecting the whole province. By no means all the provincial councils are known to us, but they must have been very numerous, even if they were not convened as often as the Nicaean canons required.

This metropolitan system, which was established quite early in the East, did not penetrate to the West until later—and then there were differences. In peninsular Italy the system never operated. In several provinces of Africa, and probably in Spain, it was the oldest bishop who held the position of metropolitan, rather than the prelate of the provincial capital. In Gaul an influential position was held by some great towns such as Arles and Marseilles which were never provincial capitals, and when in 398 the Council of Turin first established the principle of metropolitan bishoprics in Gaul, a special exception was made to the advantage of these two sees (though for Marseilles it was only temporary). As for Britain and the Danubian regions, no information is available.

PRIMATIAL SEES AND PATRIARCHATES

After the beginning of the Byzantine Empire the provinces had been divided up and multiplied, and above them the emperors had brought into being new units which were called "dioceses", there being eventually fifteen of these dioceses for the whole Empire. They were all the more convenient for use in ecclesiastical organization since most of them coincided with natural regions, later to become clearly defined nations—Spain, Britain, Africa, Egypt, etc. In this way the bishopric of Rome always remained the sole metropolitan see of "suburbican" Italy (the main peninsula and its neighbouring islands)—a relic of the time when the motherland of the Empire had not yet been divided into provinces. So too the prelates of the six African provinces were subject to the authority of the bishop of Carthage, who often presided over "plenary" councils for the whole of Africa. In Egypt the bishop of Alexandria was in effect the ecclesiastical king of the entire country, holding a position often compared to that of a Pharaoh—a time-honoured Alexandrian prerogative which was ratified in one of the canons of Nicaea and reaffirmed by the Council of Constantinople in 381. This council gave formal autonomy to the new diocesan units, at least in the Eastern Empire (Egypt, the East or Syria, Asia, Pontus, Thrace), but it did not allow the prelate of the diocesan capital a supra-provincial authority, except at Alexandria and Antioch. It was in the fifth century that the function of the "primate" began to gain in importance over the metropolitans: in the East he was known as a "patriarch", a title given to the bishops of Constantinople (which eventually included the three dioceses of Thrace, Asia and Pontus), Alexandria, Antioch, and Jerusalem. (The last-named see became a patriarchate in 451 at the expense of Antioch, which in 431 had already lost the Churches of Cyprus, henceforward "autocephalous".) In the West, besides the traditional primacies of Rome in Italy and of Carthage in Africa, a special position was gradually acquired at the end of the fourth century by western Illyricum, a district comprising the dioceses of Macedonia and Dacia, which even after its political incorporation into the Eastern Empire retained its allegiance to the ecclesiastical authority of the West: the bishop of Thessalonica held the title of "vicar apostolic", an evident case of authority delegated by the bishop of Rome, the true "patriarch of the West".

THE PAPACY

No other bishop enjoyed a status comparable to that of the

Roman pontiff, the holder of the "Apostolic See" (a title in common use after the end of the fourth century, in memory of its founder, the Prince of the Apostles). What was the range and effectiveness of this primacy? In Italy the "pope" (to use a name at first given to all important bishops and only gradually restricted to Rome) held the position of sole and unchallenged metropolitan, and most of the early Roman councils in the fourth and fifth centuries were simply assemblies of the Italian bishops, dealing with local affairs. His jurisdiction over the remainder of the West received precise formulation when in 343 the Council of Sardica provided for the possibility of appealing from a provincial sentence to Rome, where the original judgement was to be either confirmed or annulled and sent back for retrial. This is the first written affirmation of a primacy of jurisdiction which till then had been based only on custom. It has indeed been pointed out that these canons were never applied, but this does not detract from the force of the declaration made by the Fathers of Sardica: "We deem it a most excellent and fitting thing that all bishops should, from their own particular provinces, refer to their head, that is to the See of the Apostle Peter."

The powers granted at Sardica were extended by the Roman Council of 378, which recognized the pope not only as entitled to judge appeals from provincial sentences but also as having immediate jurisdiction over the metropolitans themselves. It was not long before the Roman pontiffs assumed authority to legislate, when they were consulted on particular points of doctrine or discipline: their rulings, or "decretals", are the first instance of that epistolary activity of the popes which later took the form of bulls and encyclicals. The earliest of these decretals may possibly have been sent by Pope Damasus in reply to the consultation of a Gallic council in 375: certainly Pope Siricius despatched one to the bishop of Tarragona in 385 and another to the bishops of Africa in 386, and later Innocent I addressed several to Gaul and Spain. This method of correspondence, prompted by circumstances, allowed the popes to assert their authority whenever they considered it necessary, and even when they are dealing simply with details about the liturgy or the conduct of clergy, it is significant that they speak always with authoritative firmness, "laying down the law" in confirming or fixing disciplinary rules.

Yet a limit was set to this authority in that the Eastern bishops did not consider themselves as owing obedience to Rome. At the councils of Constantinople (381) and Chalcedon (451) the primacy of "old Rome" was recognized, but only as a primacy of honour, and the see of Constantinople laid claim to second place in the Church. The argument, that Constantinople was the "new Rome", heir to the ancient capital, did less than justice to the claims of a see founded by the Prince of the Apostles. The twenty-eighth canon of Chalcedon was never recognized by Pope Leo I, whose legates had vainly protested against it, and similarly in the seventh century the Quinisextum Council (692), whose thirty-sixth canon assigned "equal privileges" both to new and old Rome, was rejected by Pope Sergius and only recognized by Constantine and John VIII with reservations referring to "enactments contrary to the ancient canons or to the ancient decrees of the holy pontiffs of this see". There is no doubt that this misunderstanding which arose in the fifth century between the Eastern Churches and the Church of Rome was the remote cause of the eleventh-century Schism.

THE COUNCILS

If we examine the ecclesiastical constitution slowly built up during this period out of ancient customs and the canons of the great councils, we can see the unity of the Church firmly established within the imperial orbit. However, taking the facts into account as well as the legalities, it must be recorded that in practice the life of the Church was often disturbed by individual outbursts, clashes of personality or group rivalries. In order to quell disorder and to restore peace, the imperial authorities sometimes took the initiative themselves, often imposing a settlement in a heavy-handed or untimely manner: otherwise the solution was the convocation of a council, assembled and presided over by a metropolitan or some other influential prelate and attended by the bishops of a group of provinces, sometimes even of large areas. The pope took a personal part only in the synods held at Rome itself, but he was represented by legates at the most important councils held outside Italy, at Arles (Constantine's assembly of all western bishops) in 314, at Nicaea (325), the first ecumenical council, also convoked at the instance of Constantine, and later again at the councils summoned by the Byzantine emperors at or near their capital: Ephesus (431), Chalcedon (451) and Constantinople (553 and 680). It was these episcopal assemblies which, often after stormy debates, settled personal or doctrinal disputes and with the aid of the "secular arm" succeeded in putting an end to schisms and heresies.

THE DONATIST SCHISM

From the time of Constantine the Donatist schism rent asunder the African Church for over a century. About 310 a party in the local Church challenged the legitimate authority of the new bishop of Carthage, Caecilian, with the accusation (a false one, as it happened) that the bishops who had carried out his election and consecration were "traditors", men who had given way under persecution. Yet there was more to the issue than a personal dispute, for beneath the surface lay regional and social antagonisms—Numidia opposed to proconsular Africa, the native proletariat opposed to the Roman landowners—which were more deep-seated than any doctrinal differences. The most important factor, when all is said and done, was African nationalism, which obstinately resisted all intervention of foreign authority, civil as well as ecclesiastical. The situation was further aggravated by the indecision of successive emperors, beginning with Constantine himself, who agreed to judge the dispute and to re-examine and retract previous verdicts: official policy oscillated continually between repression, which provoked the extremists, and toleration, which provided them with opportunities for propaganda—so well exploited that with the support of the rural banditry (or Circumcellions), and of Berber rebels such as Firmus and Gildon, the Donatists eventually succeeded in setting up a separate schismatical Church represented by hundreds of bishops, at least as numerous as their Catholic counterparts, in all the districts of Africa.

After a period of internal division (three or four rival sects were in existence at the end of the fourth century) the movement re-united in common cause against the Catholics, many of whom it alienated from the fold. Condemnations issued from the Churches of Europe, from Pope Melchiades in 313, and from the Council of Arles in 314, but against such stubbornness these were ineffectual. Before the affair could be brought to a final close at the beginning of the fifth century much more was required: the unremitting activity of St Augustine in word and writing, and above all the vigorous enforcement of the edicts of proscription issued in 411 by the emperor Honorius. In spite of its tenacity the schism remained nevertheless purely local, and with the one exception of a Donatist community which for a time maintained itself in the heart of the African colony at Rome, it never gained a footing elsewhere in the Christian world. The spirit of nationalism in the African Church (a phenomenon which had appeared as early as the time of St Cyprian in the third century) vigorously resisted further attempts at intervention by Roman authority, such as the ill-advised interference of Pope Zosimus in 417. In the latter case, however, the early decease of the pope and the tact of St Augustine combined to avert a serious crisis.

THE WESTERN CHURCHES

In the other Western Churches separation was not so evident as in Africa. But in 386 the execution of the heretic Priscillian at the orders of the emperor Maximus led to an outbreak of schism in Gaul and Spain, where St Martin, the bishop of Tours, and several other rigorist bishops, out of indignation at this interference by secular authority and as a protest against the shedding of blood, broke off relations with their fellow-bishops who had instigated or abetted the crime, namely Itacius of Ossonoba in Spain and Felix of Trier in Gaul (whence the name "Itacian" or "Felician" schism). After a breach of communion lasting several years, unity was re-established in Gaul after the Council of Turin (398) and in Spain after the Council of Toledo (400), due to the combined initiative of the pope and the bishop of Milan.

For a time the see of Milan almost challenged the Holy See's position as rightful head of the Western Church. The factors mainly responsible for this temporary ascendancy were the city's status as imperial capital between 381 and 402 and the outstanding episcopate (374–97) of St Ambrose. A former civil servant, St Ambrose was not a man to brook opposition and he had little hesitation in intervening in spheres outside his own. Besides exercising a powerful influence upon the policy of the emperors, as we have seen above, he also frequently concerned himself with ecclesiastical affairs outside his own Cisalpine provinces, intervening now in Illyria and the East to combat the effects of the Arian crisis, and now in Gaul and Spain in order to reconcile bishops. This Milanese "primacy" did not long survive the death of Ambrose and the departure, slightly later, of the imperial court.

Arles, too, claimed primatial rights under its bishops Patroclus (411–26) and St Hilary (431–49). Here again the situation was brought about by the increased importance of the town itself (now the capital of a praetorian province and the seat of a usurper) and the ambitious designs of practical intriguers like the unscrupulous and disreputable Patroclus, who even succeeded in enlisting the support of Pope Zosimus. When the latter attempted to set Patroclus over the four provinces of south-east Gaul and even to make him a sort of vicar-apostolic for the whole country, the bishops of Vienne, Narbonne and (in particular) Marseilles, resisted stoutly, and disputes continued even after the death of Zosimus and Patroclus. Claims to similar and even more extensive territorial jurisdiction were also made by Hilary of Arles, who was eventually deprived of his metropolitan title by Pope Leo in 445, and the restoration four years later only assigned to his successor a limited territory south of the province of Vienne.

THE EASTERN CHURCHES

St Leo the Great (the first pope to be so called) had been

enabled by circumstances to extend a sovereign authority over all the West, even as far as Africa, where the temporary eclipse of the see of Carthage after the Vandal persecution facilitated his intervention in Mauretania. In the East, however, in spite of his victory for orthodoxy at Chalcedon, the Roman primacy carried little weight. At the beginning of the Arian crisis in the fourth century the Alexandria of Athanasius, in her need for support against Antioch and Constantinople, had formed an alliance with Rome, but this alignment only succeeded in bringing the Roman claims under suspicion elsewhere in the East. Open cleavage came in 343 with the two rival councils of Sardica hurling excommunication at each other, the whole of the East (except for Athanasius) solidly ranged against the West. Even the settlement of the doctrinal issues did not close the breach, for although by 370 most of the Eastern Churches had returned to orthodoxy they were prevented from re-establishing communion with Rome and the West by the outbreak of the Antiochian schism. This was occasioned by two rival claimants to the see of Antioch, both orthodox, the one recognized by all the East, the other stoutly maintaining his rights in spite of the irregularity of his appointment. This stumbling-block was eventually removed at the end of the century. Subsequent controversy was nourished from one constant source, the deep-seated antagonism between Constantinople and Alexandria, an antagonism fanned into flame by any little act of individual tactlessness or doctrinal error, and more often than not fostered by the Egyptian "Pharaoh", Cyril of Alexandria. Cyril spared no effort of intrigue to secure the overthrow of St John Chrysostom in 404 and of Nestorius in 431, and in 449 his successor Dioscorus brought the same pressure to bear against the patriarch Flavian—only to meet his own downfall at Chalcedon in 451.

All this strife was but the sign of deeper ethnical and national tensions. Both the Copts of Egypt and the Syrians of Antioch were growing restive under the domination of official Hellenism and for these peoples, now developing their own national cultures, the Church tended to be identified with the imperialistic ascendancy. The same spirit of nationalism which had inspired

Byzantine caesaropapism in its defiant challenging of the Western papacy was now rousing Egypt and Syria to assert their independence against the Byzantine patriarch—with equally disastrous results. While the first movement prepared the ground for the great schism between East and West, the second tended to separate from the Empire the Coptic and Syrian Churches which were eventually swamped beneath the tide of Islam in the seventh century.

CHAPTER III

DOGMA AND HERESIES

Like the occasions of State intervention, ecclesiastical disputes were most frequently concerned with doctrinal controversies. Though the spectacle they offer is equally distressing for the display of wrangling in which a great many theologians and churchmen took delight, yet one should not turn away in disgust nor condemn these men too hastily; there was more to it than simple savage polemics or tiresome hair-splitting: the impassioned feelings let loose often sprang from an intense concern for the pursuit of truth, and slowly in the midst of this agitation was taking place the hammering-out and establishment of Catholic dogma.

THE DONATIST HERESY

We have seen that the first conflict which broke out on the morrow of the Peace of the Church had the appearance simply of a personal feud; the Donatist affair nevertheless was at least implicitly based on a doctrinal issue, characteristic of its African milieu in which a similar problem had arisen in the previous century. The validity of the consecration of the bishop Caecilian was being challenged by those who alleged that the consecrating bishops had been apostates. The schismatics were persistent in their claim to be "the Church of the Saints", as opposed to "the Church of the Traditors": in their view, sacraments conferred by unworthy persons were deprived of all validity, and consequently it was necessary to break completely with a clergy corrupted by contact with sinners, and to rebaptize or reordain those of the faithful or clergy who had failed in their allegiance. The fact that this point of view was fairly widespread among the Christians of Africa explains the initial success of Donatism, but its consequences caused repercussions abroad: in 314 the Council of Arles, in accordance with Roman tradition, declared ordinations performed by sinners to be valid, and forbade the renewal of baptism for converted heretics provided that the original baptism had been administered in the name of the Holy Trinity. Henceforward this doctrine of the sacraments was accepted by the African Catholics, and it was no longer called in question.

THE ARIAN HERESY

The controversies which rent asunder the entire Christian world during the fourth and fifth centuries involved the most fundamental problems of theology, principally the doctrine of the Blessed Trinity. Since the end of the second century two tendencies had emerged: the first, intent on safeguarding the unity of the divine nature, made the Son and the Holy Spirit simply "modes" of the Godhead: the second, seeking to maintain the distinction of the divine persons, represented the Son (whom it identified with the Platonic Logos) as a created being, the first of all creatures but subordinate to the Father. The former tendency had given birth to Modalism, the heresy of Noëtus, Praxeas and Sabellius, which was condemned at Smyrna and Rome at the beginning of the third century. With the latter tendency, called Subordinationism, were associated Tertullian, Hippolytus and Origen in varying degrees, and at the beginning of the fourth century it was revived in a more emphatic form by Lucian, a priest of Antioch, and maintained by his disciple, an Alexandrian priest named Arius. According to Arius the Word had not been begotten of the substance of the Father, but created out of nothing: there had been a time when the Word was not yet in existence, and he had been freely created by the one and eternal God who, foreseeing his merits, had adopted him as his Son.

In effect Arius' doctrine did away with the divinity of Christ, the Incarnation of the Word, and also of the Holy Spirit which proceeds from the Word. It was condemned about 320 by the bishops of Egypt assembled in council at Alexandria, but the bishops of Bithynia and Palestine, several of whom had been disciples of Lucian of Antioch, rallied in councils round Eusebius of Nicomedia and Eusebius of Caesarea to give it their support. Enthusiasm for these theological issues swept the East, and a general council was already being projected when in 325 Constantine, taking the conduct of the affair into his own hands, convoked at Nicaea in Bithynia the first ecumenical council. At Nicaea the influence of the Western Ossius of Cordova was decisive, and the official formulas clearly rejected Arianism as heretical: they proclaimed the faith of the Church in one single God, Father, Son and Holy Ghost—Jesus Christ being the Son of God, begotten and not created, consubstantial (*homoousios*) with the Father.

ARIANISM AND ITS PHASES

That was the end of the affair, it seemed, but due to the emperor's vacillation and the fickleness of his successors it was only a new beginning. The defeated party, at first deposed and exiled, soon raised its head again. The most adept at intrigue was Eusebius of Nicomedia, who lost no time in winning back Constantine's favour: it was he who baptized the emperor on his deathbed; shortly afterwards he had himself translated to the see of Constantinople, the new capital of the East. The revenge of the "Eusebians" was complete when they had successfully removed most of the Nicaean prelates: Eustathius of Antioch after 330, then Marcellus of Ancyra (suspected of Sabellianism) and above all the chief abomination of the Arians, Athanasius of Alexandria. Fifteen out of the forty-five years of his episcopate Athanasius spent in exile, twice being banished to the West by Constantine and by Constantius II, and twice compelled to flee into the desert under the same Constantius and under Julian. Because Pope Julius and the West would not recognize his deposition the Eastern Church severed relations with the members of the Roman Council of 340 and with those of the Council of Sardica in 343; it was to secure his deposition that between 353 and 356 Constantius II assembled councils at Arles, Milan and Béziers, also exiling the opposition—Hilary of Poitiers, Ossius of Cordova and Pope Liberius among them.

At this juncture, thirty years after Nicaea, a new dogma was enforced by imperial decree, but agreement on its formulations was not easily reached: three successive councils of Sirmium, meeting in 357, 358, 359, adopted widely divergent texts. The first gave expression to the radical form of Arianism, Anomoeanism, that is, the assertion, according to the views of Aetius of Antioch, of a complete dissimilarity between the Father and the Son. The second council issued a much more modified doctrine, compatible even with orthodox teaching: the only difference was that it avoided the disputed term *homoousios* (consubstantial) and substituted the term *homoiousios* (similar in substance). In the following year, however, this *homoiousianism* of Basil of Ancyra was to give way in its turn to a rather colourless compromise whereby the Son was simply similar (*homoeos*) to the Father. This was the formula the emperor settled on, and it was ratified under pressure by two general councils, summoned at Rimini for the West and at Seleucia in Isauria for the East. Throughout the Empire "homoean" Arianism was enforced as the State religion.

This "overthrow of orthodoxy" was of short duration: after 360 the accession of the Emperor Julian in the West allowed the bishops of Gaul to rally the forces of Catholic dogma, and the death of Constantius in the following year brought a universal restoration of religious liberty, to the advantage of the Nicaean or *homoousian* party in the West and of the *homoeousians* or semi-Arians in the East. In Italy and Illyria the tolerant policy of Valentinian I allowed the survival of a few isolated Arian bishops, but their death (at Milan in 374 and at Sirmium in 378) marked the final restoration of orthodoxy. In the East a development in understanding brought about a reconciliation of Catholics and semi-Arians on the basis of clarified formulas; even Athanasius approved the term "three hypostases in one essence" (hypostasis being taken in the sense of person rather than of substance), and the Cappadocian theologians, led by Basil of Caesarea, with their penetrating analyses gave new depth to Trinitarian dogma. Homoeism enjoyed a brief extension of power under Valentinian's brother, the Emperor Valens, who once more exiled the Nicaean bishops, but at his death in 378 heresy, now deprived of official support, collapsed. At Constantinople orthodoxy enjoyed a brilliant restoration under the Cappadocian Gregory of Nazianzus, and the council convoked in the Eastern capital in 381 considered it sufficient to pronounce a general anathema on Eunomians (Anomoeans), Eudoxians (Homoeans), Pneumatomachians) (semi-Arians who denied the divinity of the Holy Spirit) as well as Sabellians. Three months later two Illyrian bishops, sole survivors of the Arianism but lately all-victorious, were condemned by an assembly of bishops from all the West at the Council of Aquileia. Thanks to the active good-will of the emperors Theodosius and Gratian, heresy had disappeared from the Empire, and only the barbarians remained its adherents: converted to Christianity by Arian bishops in the time of Constantius and Valens they were to remain loyal to the faith of their fathers for two more centuries.

THE PELAGIAN HERESY

For thirty years at the turn of the century (c. 400), throughout the Christian world there was a lull in doctrinal controversy: the Priscillianist dispute in Spain and Gaul was not so much concerned with theology as with liturgical practice and moral ideas; in the East the Origenist controversy, in which Epiphanius of Salamis and St Jerome were ranged against John of Jerusalem and Rufinus of Aquileia, involved the orthodoxy of a notable third-century exegete, without raising any new problems for theologians. It was about 410 that a dispute started in Africa, spreading later to Palestine and Rome, about notions which were essential to faith. This new heresy has always remained associated with the name of the Breton Pelagius. Pelagianism was based on a very respectable moral rigorism, but its anxiety to champion man's free will and to urge him on to sanctity resulted in its denying original sin and the necessity of divine grace: for the

Pelagian, access to the Kingdom is made possible by baptism, and since perfect sanctity is an obligation and a possibility for everyone, it rests with each individual Christian to merit eternal life by his conduct, modelled on the precepts and example of Christ. Pelagius himself, an austere director of souls who by the power of his preaching and the radiance of his virtue enjoyed an extraordinary prestige and influence, always managed to avoid scandal or censure by qualifying or modifying his thought: for a long time he taught at Rome as a private teacher, and (as is shown by the first attitude of Pope Zosimus in 417) he left behind him there after his departure in 410 even more personal admirers than supporters of his views: at Jerusalem, where he had taken refuge in 415, he succeeded at the price of adroit concessions in clearing himself of charges of heresy; later, condemned by pope and councils, he seems to have found asylum in an Egyptian monastery where he died about 425. In the hands of his disciples, however, first Celestius and then Julian of Eclanum, Pelagian doctrine became more drastic and rigid: henceforward it aroused opposition and anathemas. At Carthage in 411 Pelagius was excommunicated for the first time: soon St Augustine appeared on the scene, with his countless polemical refutations and constructive treatises: it was the anti-Pelagian controversy which was the cause of the great African bishop's becoming the "Doctor of Grace". From texts of St Paul, principally the Epistle to the Romans, he reasoned out with precise logic his theory of man's fall, the flesh and its sinful lust, and salvation by sanctifying grace. His doctrine was adopted by the African councils of Carthage and Milevum in 416 and 418, by Pope Innocent, and finally in the *Tractoria* of the latter's successor Zosimus. In 418 the Emperor Honorius in his turn came out against the heresy.

All was not finished, however. After Pelagius had withdrawn into silence and Celestius had fled into hiding, the cause was sustained by Julian of Eclanum, supported by eighteen Italian bishops and some others in Gaul, Britain and Illyria. The anonymous "Declaration of Aquileia" and Julian's own writings levelled charges of Manicheism against the Augustinian doctrine of original sin and claimed to restore five "honours" flouted by the anti-Pelagians—those of the creator, marriage, the old Law, free will, and the saints. But the Pelagian bishops in the West, disowned by the Church and persecuted by the State, could not maintain the heresy for long after its condemnation and within a few years they were forced to retract or to abandon their sees. Some fled to the East where they were again condemned in 431 at the Council of Ephesus, and at that point Pelagianism disappears from the scene.

On the other hand "Augustinism", as developed in St Augustine's later treatises, did not go unopposed among orthodox theologians, some of whom saw in its insistence upon the depth of concupiscence and the terrible consequences of original sin a danger of underestimating the effects of the redemption. Grace exalted at the expense of free will, irreconcilable opposition between the "predestined" and the *massa perditionis*—did not all this amount to fatalism and a denial of human freedom? So it seemed at least to Cassian and the school of Lérins (the leaders of monastic thought in Gaul, later known as "semi-Pelagians") who became engaged in long controversy with St Augustine's vigorous defender Prosper of Aquitaine. Ecclesiastical authority long refrained from committing itself on the issue, and when St Augustine died (430) Pope Celestine confined himself to paying tribute to the learning and merits of the great saint. A council of Arles in 475 condemned the priest Lucidius for predestinationism, and a treatise of bishop Faustus of Riez "On the grace of God and free will" was to show the human soul as containing the image of God, having not only an undeniable inclination towards sin but also a certain natural desire of the good. The final Catholic doctrine on grace and original sin, as promulgated at the Council of Orange in 529 and ratified by Pope Boniface II in 531, was to reproduce the main outlines of the Augustinian theory, purged of exaggerated and polemical expressions.

THE NESTORIAN HERESY

The primary purpose of the Council of Ephesus, which virtually dealt Pelagianism its death-blow in 431, had been to settle the Christological controversies prevailing in the East. The theological passions of these Eastern Churches ever ran high where speculation about the Godhead was concerned, while by comparison little interest was aroused by the doctrines of man and his destiny: with Arianism in the fourth century the main issue had turned on the three persons of the Trinity, while from the fifth century the person and natures of Christ became the centre of interest. In both controversies alike the Western Church proved almost entirely unreceptive to the subtle distinctions elaborated by the Greek theologians.

From the first, Christians had recognized the existence of two elements in the person of Jesus, divine and human. The question was, how to define this duality. A solution quickly rejected was that of the Docetists, who made Christ's humanity simply an appearance. A similar heresy maintained by the Syrian bishop Apollinaris of Laodicea in the fourth century equated the human nature of Jesus with his body (the divine Word taking the place of the soul), but this doctrine, which left our Lord only with one, divine, nature was condemned in 377 by Pope Damasus and in 381 by the first Council of Constantinople. A reaction against Apollinaris set in with the theology of the Antiochene school, particularly as formulated by the two Cilician bishops, Diodore of Tarsus and Theodore of Mopsuestia, who taught the coexistence of two natures, and even of two persons, in Christ— the man Jesus and the Word, substantially distinct even though closely united by the Incarnation. This was the doctrine introduced to Constantinople from Antioch in 428 by the newly appointed patriarch Nestorius. This high-minded, heresy-hunting prelate made a disastrous attempt to prohibit the monks and clergy of the capital from applying the title *Theotokos* to the Virgin Mary, whom he held to be the mother of Christ but not of God. Rioting broke out at Constantinople and Cyril, patriarch of Alexandria, eagerly seizing the opportunity of striking down his hated rival, opened a campaign of intrigue in ecclesiastical and political circles which ended with the condemnation of Nestorius by Pope Celestine, by the ecumenical council of Ephesus in 431, and, finally, by the emperor at Constantinople. Cyril's formulas were themselves not above suspicion as we shall see and they aroused the opposition of the Syrian bishops. Nestorius eventually accepted the term Theotokos after certain precisions had been obtained, but his mischievous character and the ill-will (not to say dishonesty) of Cyril made any real confrontation of their respective positions quite impossible. The patriarch of Antioch had originally been included in the condemnation of Nestorius and after the latter's removal all the diplomacy of pope and emperor was necessary before he could be reconciled with his rival at Alexandria. By a proclamation of 433 the two natures were declared to be united without confusion—a compromise based on an Antiochene formula but made possible by the favourite Alexandrian idea of the "communication of idioms", that is, the reciprocal exchange between the two natures of the properties belonging to each.

THE EUTYCHIAN HERESY

Alexandria, however, was not satisfied with this compromise agreement and after several years the new Egyptian patriarch Dioscorus took up the struggle once more, enlisting support at Constantinople from the monastic party, led by the Archimandrite Eutyches, and from sympathizers at Court. In 448 the condemnation of Nestorius was reiterated by an imperial law which ordered the deposition of his supporters and proclaimed the orthodoxy of Cyril's writings. The other side replied by challenging the orthodoxy of the aged Eutyches, accused of denying Christ's humanity which he had declared to be absorbed into his divinity "like a drop of honey in the water of the sea". Found guilty and excommunicated by a synod of Constantinople, Eutyches appealed to Pope Leo and obtained support from the Court which at Ephesus (449) assembled a new council, again dominated by the Alexandrian patriarch. Here the old Apollinarian formula "One incarnate nature of the divine Word" was reproduced as "Two natures before the union, one nature after it"—a statement of pure and simple Monophysitism which was forced on the assembled bishops by the intrigue and bullying of

Dioscorus, supported by imperial officialdom and mob pressure. Flavian of Constantinople was deposed, and also the principal Antiochene theologians Ibas of Edessa, Irenaeus of Tyre and Theodoret of Cyrrhus. "The Robber Council" someone called it at the time, and the name has remained ever since.

A protest from Pope Leo, whose legates had remained powerless and even culpably passive during the proceedings, was in vain, for Theodosius immediately ratified all the decrees of Ephesus. Orthodoxy was not lost, however, for the emperor was killed in an accident soon afterwards and his successor proved favourable to the Roman position. The Council of Chalcedon in 451 rehabilitated the victims of the "Robber Council", excommunicated and deposed Dioscorus and finally defined the Catholic faith in terms which corresponded to Leo's formulation in the famous "Letter to Flavian".

[Jesus Christ was declared to be] complete in divinity and complete in humanity—truly God and truly man, composed of a rational soul and a body—consubstantial with the Father in his divinity and consubstantial with us in his humanity, similar to us in all things save sin—in his divinity begotten of the Father before all ages, and in his humanity born in this last age for us and for our salvation of the Virgin Mary, Mother of God—subsisting in two natures which are unmixed and unchanged, undivided and unseparated, since far from the distinction of natures being destroyed in the union, the qualities of each are preserved and both are united in one Person and one hypostasis.

THE MONOPHYSITE HERESY AND ITS PHASES

The Christological definition of Chalcedon was as clear and unequivocal as the Trinitarian definition of Nicaea had been in the previous century. But now as then the conciliar decree did not mean the termination of the conflict, and indeed the Monophysite crisis proved to be even more lengthy and serious than its Arian predecessor. In Egypt and Syria, as we have seen, the Monophysite opposition was firmly entrenched, thanks to a measure of imperial favour and the spirit of nationalism.

Attempts at compromise only aggravated the situation. The first was the *Henoticon* or edict of union issued by the Emperor Zeno (482) which reaffirmed the principles of Nicaea and Ephesus and the condemnations of Nestorius and Eutyches but at the same time accepted Cyril's anathemas and left the whole question of natures undefined. Since the declaration ended by anathematizing all who had expressed different opinions "whether at Chalcedon or at any other council", it is not surprising that it met with a flat rejection from Pope Felix III, who excommunicated those Eastern patriarchs who had given it their assent. The extreme Monophysites on the other hand found the document too moderate and only acquiesced after pressure from the emperor (first Zeno and later Anastasius). Severus at Antioch was only one of the many heretics who now came to power in the Churches of Egypt and Syria under cover of this union by constraint.

Orthodoxy was restored in 519 but later Justinian, instigated by the Empress Theodora and intent on reinforcing unity at all costs, initiated a fresh attempt at compromise with the solemn "condemnation" (544) of the "Three Chapters", writings of the three fifth-century theologians Theodore of Mopsuestia, Ibas of Edessa and Theodoret of Cyrrhus. The first of these was a Nestorian before Nestorius, uncondemned in his lifetime, while the two others, convicted at the Robber Council of Ephesus but reinstated at Chalcedon after an affirmation of the crucial texts and a repudiation of Nestorianism, still remained the first objects of hatred to the Monophysites, whom the emperor now hoped to bring back to the official Church by publicly disavowing the "heretics". In 553 an imperial council at Constantinople ratified the condemnation of the Three Chapters in spite of opposition from Pope Vigilius, but even the latter finally assented and his successor Pelagius contrived precariously to combine fidelity to the decisions of Chalcedon with submissiveness to the emperor's Caesaropapism. Yet Justinian's efforts were wasted. The Monophysites remained unyielding in their hostility to Chalcedon and to the imperial Church (the "Melchite" Church, as it was called in Semitic countries) and though officially excluded from all episcopal sees they set up a clandestine Church under the protection of Theodora herself. The apostle of the sect was James, a monk known from his tattered dress as Baradai, or the Ragman, who after becoming bishop *in partibus* of Edessa travelled up and down the East consecrating bishops and ordaining priests and deacons—to an estimated number of more than a hundred thousand, including nearly thirty bishops. The result was the establishment of a complete dissident hierarchy (notably at Alexandria and Antioch) known after its founder as "Jacobite", which was enabled by the support of the monks and the fanatical mob to survive all police persecution.

The Monophysites were weakened not so much by persecution, however, as by the internal divisions which soon appeared in their own ranks. The original Eutychians were challenged by a party known as Severians after a Monophysite Patriarch of Antioch who held that the single nature of the Incarnate Word still retained the properties of the divine and human natures. The Julianists, disciples of Julian of Halicarnassus, then broke away from the Severians, maintaining the incorruptibility of Christ's body as a result of his exemption from original sin—a doctrine which, though capable of an orthodox interpretation, laid itself open to a complete Docetism which would deny the actuality of the Passion. At the end of his reign Justinian formed the ambitious project of reconciling all the various trends by enforcing this last doctrine, commonly called "Aphthartodocetism", but he succeeded merely in arousing the indignation of Severians and supporters of Chalcedon alike, and only the emperor's death (565) prevented the outbreak of fresh disorders. Last came the Tritheists, with their teaching that for every person in the Trinity there is "a corresponding nature, substance and divinity": John Philoponus, the leader of this sect, maintained the Aristotelian doctrine that not only nature and person, but also form and matter, are inseparable—a view fatal to the resurrection since the destruction of the body's form must mean the destruction of its matter also. Of Philoponus' disciples, Athanasius accepted his inferences on the resurrection while Conon upheld only his Trinitarian teaching. By the end of the sixth century, with these splinter groups of Eutychians, Julianists (or Phantasiasts), Athanasians and Cononists, and with Alexandria in schism with Antioch, Monophysitism presented a picture of complete disintegration, and the spiritual morale of the people had been gravely undermined. This was the situation in these provinces under the sway of heresy on the eve of the successive Persian and Arab invasions.

MONENERGISM AND MONOTHELITISM

The emperor Heraclius considered this a propitious moment for restoring unity between all the Churches on the basis of a formula acceptable to Monophysites and Catholics alike. The formula selected for the purpose was "unity of theandric operation" or "Monenergism" (from the Greek word ἐνέργεια), a term logically following from the idea of one nature and already defended by the Monophysite Severus of Antioch, but which had been cunningly juxtaposed with the Chalcedonian definition of two natures by the adroit Sergius of Constantinople. The finished product seemed to the emperor unexceptionable, and by 630 he had obtained the assent of the Monophysites of Antioch under Anastasius the Camel Driver, and those of Alexandria under Cyrus of Phasis. But in less than ten years the invasion of the Caliphs cut these Churches off from the rest of Christendom, thereby providing their Monophysite prelates with a welcome release from Byzantine authority and enabling them to pursue their heretical doctrines undisturbed under infidel rule.

Even before the Mohammedan victories, however, there was a movement of resistance to Monenergism in Palestine. Sophronius, a monk who became patriarch of Jerusalem in 634, protested against the equivocations of court theology and in a vigorous profession of faith proclaimed a twofold natural operation in Christ, to ensure the distinction of natures, "whose union is without confusion. For natures are recognized by their operations, and diversity of operations shows a diversity of essences." This opposition provoked the Patriarch Sergius to a public reply: arguments about one or two operations were fruitless, he said, since these expressions were not found in the Fathers, and he induced Pope Honorius to take the same position with the statement that "our Saviour, the one Jesus Christ, performed in his two natures the acts of his divinity and the acts of his humanity". · The pope refused, however, to assert either one or two "operations"—regarding the one term as tainted with Nestorianism, the other with Eutychianism—and he insisted on the one single person who acts in two distinct natures. Sergius also persuaded the emperor of his policy, and it was he who composed the *Ecthesis* (638) promulgated by Honorius as a State decree and ratified forthwith by a council of Constantinople. In this, the faith of Byzantine Christendom was officially defined in the following terms: "The activities proper to God and the activities proper to man proceed from the single identity of the one Incarnate God, the Word, without confusion or division, and are predicated of one and the same subject." Dismissing the terms "one operation" and "two operations" as equally inappropriate, the imperial decree then went on with the assertion: "our Lord Jesus Christ has but one will". This change of one word, replacing Monenergism by Monothelitism, obviously could not satisfy the defenders of orthodoxy. The year 638 saw the death of all the main protagonists, Sophronius, Sergius and Honorius, and the next pope, Severinus, refused to sanction the *Ecthesis*—unequivocal condemnation following from his successor John IV and Theodore, and from the bishops of Africa. Finally at the great Council of the Lateran assembled by Pope Martin I in 649, the Catholic faith was defined in terms which excluded both Monenergism and Monothelitism alike; "There are in our Lord not only two natures, unmixed in their union, but also two natural wills, the divine will and the human will, and two natural operations, the divine operation and the human operation. He is our truly one Lord and God, Jesus Christ, at once perfect God and perfect man, who has both divinely and humanly willed and operated our salvation."

This council came only a year after the promulgation of the *Typos*, an edict issued by the emperor Constans II at the instance of the patriarch Paul, which had forbidden under pain of severe punishments all further discussion or controversy about the question of one or two wills or operations. Defiant, Martin now flayed heresy with his anathemas and in a universal encyclical denounced "the impious Ecthesis and the yet more impious Typos", while the emperor retaliated by subjecting him to monstrous brutalities. It was thirty years before agreement was finally reached in the Church. Then, in the sixth ecumenical Council of Constantinople held in 681, in the presence of the Emperor Constantine IV and the legates of Pope Agatho, the previous rulings on Monenergism and Monothelitism received solemn confirmation for which there was immediate and general support. Monothelitism had been dealt a fatal blow. A revival was attempted by the Emperor Philippicus in 711 but he was deposed after a few months and orthodoxy was restored in 713 by his successor Anastasius II. Only the monks of St Maron in the Lebanon refused to accept the decisions of Constantinople, which they regarded as tainted with Nestorianism—a misunderstanding which lasted until the "Maronites" were finally reconciled with the Church of Rome in the twelfth century.

The sixth ecumenical council marks the close of the great era of Christological controversy. While the Eastern Fathers derived evident satisfaction from their inclusion of Pope Honorius in the general condemnation of the Monothelites, they gladly declared that "Peter has spoken through Agatho". In the sphere of faith there was complete agreement between East and West, and the doctrine worked out by the six great councils now possessed an authority which no one was to dispute.

CHAPTER IV

CHRISTIAN LIFE

This study of theological systems in conflict and of dogma in the making has introduced us into the interior life of the Church in a way that our account of ecclesiastical organization and of political struggles failed to do. Yet, as a rule, these controversies only concerned the ruling class or an educated *élite*. What of the great mass of Christians, folk leading ordinary religious lives far removed from the great affairs of princes, prelates or doctors? This everyday aspect of our history is the most intractable of all, due to the scarcity of explicit documentation, but some attempt must be made to bring it to life if we are to have any idea of the Christian past.

RELIGIOUS ART

Churches may be said to give the religious life its external framework, and in the period following the persecutions church architecture underwent remarkably widespread developments. The secret assemblies furtively held in private houses or, more rarely, in the underground catacomb cemeteries, were now memories of the past. Many churches on the small scale had sprung up since the third century but now, under Constantine, they were no longer considered sufficient; besides, many had been destroyed in accordance with the ruthless policy of Diocletian and hence needed rebuilding.

The Roman catacombs therefore ceased to be used as places of assembly and even as a burial ground—save for certain privileged persons who sought a resting-place with the martyrs. However, a work of restoration and embellishment was undertaken about

370 by Pope Damasus, for the benefit of devout Romans and pilgrims whose scratched *graffiti* are still to be seen today; even later evidence of fifth- and sixth-century frescoes depicting our Lady and the saints shows how long this assiduous piety persisted. The popularity of the Catacombs only began to wane in the eighth and ninth centuries: after 817, however, when Pope Pascal II ordered the removal of more than two thousand bodies to the Pantheon, they were abandoned and indeed forgotten.

The new places of worship at Rome and everywhere else took the form of vast basilicas, erected on open ground or against the ramparts of the town. The word basilica was originally used of civic buildings, whose main characteristics were now reproduced in the shape of a rectangle divided lengthwise into three parallel naves, with a vestibule at one end and an apse at the other, and topped by a sloping roof. The arrangement had, however, already been used by the Christians as well as by other sects and although none of these earlier basilicas has survived intact, owing to the systematic devastations of the persecutors, we may assume that the new constructions were modelled on the old, since the historian Eusebius states that "Constantine erected new edifices on a much larger scale than their predecessors ... taller and more imposing". The original plan can still be seen, notwithstanding later reconstructions, in the great Roman basilicas like St Mary Major and St Paul's outside the Walls and in the great sixth-century basilicas of Ravenna, S. Apollinare Nuovo and S. Apollinare in Classe. Similar churches, though smaller and containing certain architectural variations, have also been excavated at sites in Africa and Syria.

Other variations were the octagonal plan, Oriental in origin, which was adopted for the baptistery of the Lateran at Rome and soon became the regular form of baptistery, and the circular plan, used by Constantine's architects for the Holy Sepulchre at Jerusalem. At Constantinople Justinian's architects produced a combination of the rotunda with a rectangular exterior: the basilica of the Holy Apostles was built in the form of a cross, while Sancta Sophia, the most splendid of all, had the exterior shape of a rectangle and the interior shape of an oval, fronted by an

atrium and narthex, mounting to a lofty rotunda fringed by gal-
leries and crowned by a massive cupola. The building's vast
dimensions (so vast as to endanger its stability: after twenty years
it caved in and had to be rebuilt) were the marvel of the contemporary world and of all succeeding generations until the fifteenth
century, when it became a Turkish mosque.

Even the boldness of line in Sancta Sophia was not so great a
wonder as its decoration—the supreme artistic achievement of
the late Christian Empire. Frescoes, so often found on the walls
of ancient buildings, civil and religious, were little used after the
time of Constantine: apart from the catacombs, the only surviving examples are at St. Clemente and St Mary Major, where between the sixth and eighth centuries many frescoes were painted
one on top of the other, representing our Lady, Christ and certain
saints. More widespread was mosaic-work, an art-form which
has survived in a better state of preservation. Mosaic had long
been used at Rome to cover the floors and later the walls of
dwelling-houses or public buildings: this practice was now continued in the new Christian buildings according to the old style
but with different subjects: the old geometrical designs, inter-
weaving patterns, animal figures and scenes from everyday life or
mythology were now replaced by symbolical representations and
the great themes of religious history, depicted alongside the
purely decorative motifs—mainly on the triumphal arch above
the choir or on the rear wall of the apse. Examples at Rome are
in the so-called mausoleum of S. Constanza, St Mary Major and
S. Pudenziana, which contain representations of Christ, our
Lady, the apostles, the animals which symbolize the evangelists
and structures evoking the heavenly Jerusalem. Other fourth-century mosaics are to be found in the cathedral of Aquileia. At
Ravenna, the mausoleum of Galla Placidia contains mosaics of
the fifth century but here the great period is the sixth century and
its monument is S. Vitale, where the apse is dominated by a royal
Christ in majesty and the walls thronged with clerical and lay
dignitaries attending the emperor and empress in solemn procession. These two great tableaux symbolize the position which
the *basileis* held in the Church, and are eminently characteristic

of contemporary religious art. The mosaics at Sancta Sophia were covered with whitewash or large scrolls to mark the advent of Mohammed and only coloured stone facing and stylized acanthus-leaf capitals survive from its original decoration, so that we must look to Ravenna now if we are to recapture the glories of the Byzantine church, in its dimensions, the colours of mosaics or precious stones, the brilliant lights reflected from hundreds of candelabra—the total effect must have been an incomparable expression of an age marked by its sense of grandeur and feeling for pomp and splendour.

THE LITURGY

Against such a background the worship of the Church was performed with supreme solemnity. Some of the original rich stateliness is still to be found in the oriental rites, though our own Roman liturgy has its share of the inheritance. The celebrant was normally the bishop, assisted by priests, deacons and other clerics whom he chose and ordained himself. Ordinations, which took place several times a year on a Sunday or the preceding night, soon began to acquire a definite ceremonial. The ancient rite used at Rome is known to us from the so-called Gelasian Sacramentary, part of which can be dated to the time of Pope Gelasius in the late sixth century. Essentially it consisted in the imposition of hands performed by the bishop, preceded by prayers of consecration composed in that precise and authoritative style so characteristic of the Roman Church. The clerics in major orders (in the West, vowed to celibacy) often lived in community with the bishop, who presided over their gatherings for worship and entrusted them with certain tasks. These gradually became more important as the number of the faithful increased. After the fifth century priests were allowed to bestow certain "sacraments": the blessing of man and wife and reception of their mutual consent, the absolution of sinners seeking penance, and the anointing of the sick with holy oil. However, the bishop still reserved to himself the administration of baptism, the principal sacrament, which was the occasion for solemn ceremonies preceded by a lengthy period of preparation. Adult baptism was almost a universal rule, for often even in Christian families application was postponed till after the "age of reason", and many tepid or cautious souls, following Constantine's example, even waited until the actual hour of death. Candidates had to undergo a period of probation and instruction called the cate-chumenate: the instruction itself was given more or less individu-ally by deacons and deaconesses, and then during Lent the bishop (or sometimes one of his assistants) delivered a series of special sermons expounding dogma and the Scriptures—catecheses often full of solid spiritual nourishment, as we can see from the extant examples, in Greek and Latin, left us by Fathers of the Church. The last week of Lent gradually evolved a fixed order. First, the knowledge of the catechumens was tested at three examinations or "scrutinies", then came the solemn recital of the Apostles' Creed and the Lord's Prayer, and finally on Easter Eve (or some-times at Pentecost) came the sacramental cleansing by immersion in the baptismal font, performed by the bishop after prayers and ritual exorcisms. The neophyte, dressed in his white robes, usually received the anointing with chrism (later "confirmation") immediately afterwards, and communicated during the Easter Mass.

The climax and centre of Christian worship was the Sunday Mass. After the second century the primitive Mass liturgy de-veloped many local variations and each of the great metropolitan sees jealously preserved and propagated its own rite within its own area. These individual liturgies deserve separate study: the rites of Antioch, Jerusalem, Alexandria and Constantinople in the East, and those of Rome, Milan, Gaul and Spain in the West. The relation between these rites, and their origins, are still the subject of specialist discussion, but it appears that Greek was the universal liturgical language throughout the East, prevailing also at Lyons till the second century and at Rome till the third: Syriac and Coptic, at first used only in the country districts of Syria and Egypt, did not become official liturgical languages in their respective provinces until the coming of the Arab invasion. The Byzantine rite eventually established throughout the Eastern Empire was probably derived from the liturgy of St James originally used at Jerusalem and Antioch. In the West, the "Gallican" liturgy has often been ascribed to Milanese origins and the Ambrosian liturgy of North Italy regarded as a fourth-century importation from the East, but recent scholarship tends to regard the different western liturgies as later variations on an earlier, uniform, rite of the first centuries whose primitive characteristics were best preserved in the Gallican usages.

Without entering into purely academic differences of detail we may certainly remark a considerable similarity in the ceremonies and sacred texts of both halves of the Christian world. In the East, preparation of the sacrificial elements to the accompaniment of prayers and incensing preceded the synaxis (Mass) itself, which then began with hymns and the Trisagion (Sanctus). After the reading of the epistle and gospel of the day, followed by a homily, came the solemn offertory procession, kiss of peace, singing of the Creed (or *Symbolum Fidei*) and the anaphora (or canon) which included an epiclesis (prayer for consecration) and ended with communion. It is evident from documents of the sixth and seventh centuries (i.e. the Leonine, Gelasian and Gregorian sacramentaries, which are really later than their eponymous popes) that the Roman Mass was made up of the same elements, only arranged in a different order. A procession came first, accompanied by the singing of a litany and the *Kyrie Eleison* (taken over from the Greeks) and followed by the sung *Gloria* (the Introit was a later, sixth-century, addition). After the so-called "collect" prayer, which varied according to the feast, came the readings which were the main elements of the Mass of the catechumens: Epistle (sometimes accompanied by a "prophecy" or text from the Old Testament) and Gospel, separated by the singing of the gradual and *alleluia* and followed by a homily. After the dismissal of the catechumens, the schola sang the offertory psalm while the bread and wine were prepared and offered and then the celebrant, after reciting the prayer over the offerings ("secret"), sang the Preface—an act of praise which did not exclude spontaneous improvisation, ending with the *Sanctus*. The text of the Canon itself, together with the words of consecration, remained substantially the same as it was in the very earliest centuries and is today. Before the sixth century the fraction preceded the Lord's Prayer, the communion came immediately after the kiss of peace, and after a final prayer the ceremony ended with the blessing. Nearly all the parts of our present-day Latin Mass can be observed in this descriptive list.

However, the rite differed from our own in a certain number of material details. Communion was received in both kinds, and the bread (not as yet simply an unleavened host) was placed in the communicant's hand, while the wine was drunk through a straw from the chalice. During the introductory part of the Mass the celebrant was seated on a raised throne surrounded by his clergy at the back of the apse: standing there to deliver the homily, he then advanced to celebrate the sacrifice facing the people over the altar (which was a simple table without cross, candles or tabernacle). Thus the ritual gestures could be followed by all, and even in the Eastern churches it was only later that the iconostasis (a high screen with curtained doors) replaced the original low grating which had marked off the choir.

The length of the eucharistic liturgy was considerable, since both psalms and prayers were usually sung by the schola and congregation and there was often a protracted homily: at Jerusalem several priests preached successively, and Hilary of Arles (fifth century) was known to speak for as long as four hours at a stretch. To judge from many accounts, the people standing in the nave moved about or fidgeted with little appearance of being recollected or prayerful.

DEVOTION TO THE SAINTS AND POPULAR PIETY

In spite of the lengthiness which was (and in the East, still is) a feature of this eucharistic service, the faithful again returned to church on certain feasts for the celebration of the vigil, a nocturnal office at which the psalms were sung antiphonally by two choirs. This custom, which originated at Antioch about the middle of the fourth century, became established in the West about the time of St Ambrose (who was the author of hymns in verse, also designed for singing).

These services gradually acquired variations according to the different seasons. The Easter cycle together with the forty days of Lent was established at an early date. The date of Easter, which in the first centuries had often been the occasion of grave conflict, was fixed each year by the Alexandrians, whose system of reckoning was extended to the whole Church by the council of Nicaea. Later there appeared also the Christmas cycle: the East celebrated the birth and baptism of Jesus on January 6th with three Masses at Bethlehem, Jerusalem and the basilica of the Resurrection, while Rome had its feast of the Nativity, held on December 25th (perhaps in order to christianize the pagan celebrations on the same day in honour of the sun god). Apostles also, and holy men and women of the Old and New Testaments, had their own feasts: SS. Peter and Paul at Rome on June 29th (probably the anniversary of a translation of their bones), the Holy Innocents on December 28th, and the Machabees on August 1st. At the beginning of the fifth century the feast of St Stephen was established on December 26th, and also the "Dormition" of the Blessed Virgin—originally held on January 18th but transferred to August 15th in the seventh century, when other Marian feasts (the Nativity, Conception and Annunciation) were instituted. The frescoes to be found in the catacombs show that the devotion to our Lady which was such a flourishing feature of the medieval age in East and West alike had already taken root in the earliest days of the Church, but it was the Nestorian controversy in the fifth century which provided its main impetus: even before 440 there were churches dedicated to the Blessed Virgin at Rome, Constantinople and Ephesus.

This period also saw the rapid development of the cultus of the saints, not as yet by any system of canonization but under the pressure of popular devotion, sanctioned by the local bishop. A feast was celebrated sometimes on the day of the saint's death, sometimes on the day of his funeral or translation of his bones, and occasionally on some other anniversary (e.g. for St Ambrose, that of his episcopal consecration). These honours had at first been restricted to martyrs, but were now extended to "confessors"—those who had practised heroic virtue or were credited with miracles worked during their lifetime or later. At an early date the faithful began to seek "pledges" of protection by venerating relics of the Lord's elect: an account from the beginning of the fourth century describes a pious Carthaginian lady as carrying the relic of a martyr on her person and kissing it before communion. Not long afterwards the empress Helena discovered in Palestine remains of the true Cross, whose fragments were soon dispersed throughout the world. The practice of cutting up the bodies of saints for export purposes must also have begun in the fourth century since it was expressly forbidden in a law of Theodosius, and St Augustine roundly condemned the trafficking to which it gave rise. It continued in the modified form of distributing pieces of linen or cloth which had touched a saint's tomb (the ordinary connotation of the word "relic" in the West) and this popular devotion received the sanction of the Church. As St Jerome puts it: "We honour the saints in order to worship him to whom they witnessed, and we honour the servants in order that this honour may redound to their Master's glory." Among the uninformed, however, this kind of piety degenerated into serious abuses—sordid trafficking, theft, or superstitions more or less taken over from paganism.

ASCETICISM AND MONASTICISM

Then as now the Christian body was not all composed of saints. As her numbers grew to include almost the whole population of the Empire, so various levels of observance began to make their appearance within the Church. In the centre came the solid block of those faithful whose religion was somewhat undeveloped and in general rather lukewarm; on one side of these were the sinners who had to be excluded from the Church, and on the other those devout souls who scrupulously cultivated the Christian virtues.

Grave public offences were punished by excommunication: the offenders were deprived of communion with the faithful, and while their penance lasted they were obliged to leave the church with the catechumens after the preliminary part of the Mass. The term of penance was fixed usually by the bishop (at Rome after the fifth century by one of the penitentiary priests), and after its completion public sinners were reconciled on the occasion of a solemn feast, usually Maundy Thursday. Sometimes the period could be curtailed, as in the case of Theodosius. In certain districts and for certain offences, notably the sin of relapse, the penance lasted until death: several fifth-century popes laid down that the lapsed were not to be refused absolution at the hour of death. The origins of private penance and its imposition for secret offences are difficult to determine, but from this period onwards we find the practice co-existing with the public form. The Church was taking up spiritual weapons against sin, ever present in mankind.

EASTERN MONASTICISM

In contrast to these defaulters, punished by a still rigorous discipline, were those Christians who set the ideal for their fellows and scaled the heights of asceticism. Sometimes it was the very sinners who had plumbed the depths of sin who became the models of heroic sanctity. Now that the end of persecution had removed the possibility of dying for Christ, the fervent Christian sought death instead through renunciation of the world and the practice of extraordinary mortifications. This ascetical way of life may be traced back to the very beginnings of Christianity, if not earlier: besides the Essene communities existing in the first century there must always have been hermits living on the confines of the Eastern desert. But the earliest known "monk" (one who lives alone) was St Antony of Egypt, who is known to us through the rather romanticized life written by St Athanasius. The anchorites of Egypt, Palestine and Syria became well-known and popular figures throughout the Christian world through the many marvellous tales written about them in the fourth and fifth centuries. In spite of the difficulty of distinguishing fact from fiction in these stories, one can discern a definite spiritual doctrine beneath the tissue of childish fables and incredible fantasies: separation from their fellow-men and the practice of rigorous fasts were seen by these monks as a means of liberation from the tyranny of the senses in order to attain divine contemplation and a foretaste on this earth of the heavenly joys to come. Yet such a life, lived in solitude under the blazing desert sun, was not without its dangers, and many of these fervent souls fell a prey to pride, singularity, and even madness.

A new form of monasticism designed to avoid these dangers was proposed in the fourth century by the Egyptian St Pachomius, the originator of the cenobitic or common life. In the first communities of men and women, which he founded in the Thebaid some distance from the Nile, discipline and authority replaced the former anchorite anarchy. Several buildings were constructed to house the individual cells, common refectory, church and outbuildings, and each house was presided over by a superior or "abbot" (father) who saw to it that the rule was observed in all its requirements: chastity, fasting, work and regular attendance at the offices. A few years later a more mitigated rule was drawn up by St Basil which laid greater emphasis on work, whether manual or intellectual, and increased the powers of the abbot in order to avoid the excesses of individual caprice. This Basilian rule eventually prevailed throughout the Byzantine Empire.

The Eastern monastic movement was by no means perfect, however, and dubious elements were not long in appearing. Numbers of "gyrovagues" left their monasteries to tramp the roads or else they flocked to the cities where they created unrest that was pernicious even if not deliberate. Many of these abuses had to be countered by imperial intervention in the name of public order, or by the bishops in the name of legitimate authority, but these ascetics (like the Stylites, with their spectacular mortifications) always enjoyed considerable prestige among the common people, who often travelled great distances in order to gaze at their heroes, to question or to admire. In all this, the West took its lessons from the East.

WESTERN MONASTICISM

The Latin world first came into contact with monasticism through St Athanasius, who spent his exile in Gaul and Italy. At the beginning monastic observances—fasting, chastity, study of

Scripture and singing of the psalms—were practised in the world. There were consecrated virgins who received a sacred veil from the bishop, and like the widows (who were formally discouraged from contracting a second marriage) they were allotted a special place in the church, but they lived separately with their own families. Men too adopted practices of piety and asceticism while remaining in the world, like the writer Sulpicius Severus in Gaul and his contemporary Paulinus, later bishop of Nola. The latter and his Spanish wife, Theresa, even separated by mutual agreement. An asceticism of extreme severity now began to appear in Spain.

This austere and rigoristic Spanish milieu was the breeding-ground for what came to be known as Priscillianism, so called after the wealthy Priscillian, later bishop of Avila, who assumed leadership of the sect. To a great extent the heresy is shrouded in mystery, both as regards the origin of the writings attributed to Priscillian and the precise bearing of his doctrine, but its fanaticism evidently took the form of a morbid taste for the apocryphal Scriptures and for extraordinary observances and secret meetings: hence arose suspicions of immorality which developed into accusations of magic and Manicheism. Several Lusitanian bishops, who seem to have been disreputable arch-schemers, persecuted the Priscillianists with implacable hostility and succeeded in having them condemned by a council at Saragossa in 380, by the emperor Gratian in 382, by a council at Bordeaux in 384 and by the emperor Maximus in 386. Finally, Priscillian and six of his companions were executed at Trier, while in Spain his followers were hunted down by an imperial commission which spread terror in its wake. This brutal violence provoked St Martin and St Ambrose to public denunciation and the whole episode (so like the later Inquisition) aroused keen indignation in Gaul and Spain from the best of the bishops, though the majority of the episcopate in both countries accepted the actions of the civil power without question. This suppression of Priscillianism seems to have been provoked partly by hostility towards the new ascetical movement, which certain excesses had rendered suspect.

To this period also belong the founders of Western monasticism,

St Ambrose and St Martin. About 380 St Ambrose, as bishop of Milan, brought his clerics together into an authentic monastic community, thereby following the example of another North Italian bishop, Eusebius of Vercelli, later imitated also by St Augustine at Hippo. Earlier still in 371, Martin, a native of Pannonia who had become an anchorite at Ligugé near Poitiers, established the first monastery in Gaul in Marmoutiers, just outside the city of Tours (of which he was later to become bishop). At the beginning of the fifth century other more lasting foundations were made in Provence, by St Honoratus on the island of Lérins and by the oriental monk John Cassian at Saint-Victor of Marseilles. Like Marmoutiers, these Provençal abbeys soon became nurseries of bishops as well as centres of asceticism; hence arose a persistent distrust of monks among ecclesiastical circles in Gaul.

We find the same hostility towards asceticism at the end of the fourth century in Rome, where the opposition was pushed by some to indefensible extremes. Helvidius went as far as to deny that our Lady remained a virgin after the birth of Jesus, and Jovinian openly disparaged celibacy and fasting which, he maintained, were no more meritorious than their opposites. These excesses were condemned by the ecclesiastical authorities. Yet the officials of the Roman Church, while not lending the slightest support to these outrageous vagaries, always remained distrustful of what was too advanced. St Jerome, whose sharp tongue did not spare the worldly clergy, aroused great animosity by acting as spiritual director to certain pious women drawn to a life of asceticism, and he was obliged to leave Rome after the death of his protector Pope Damasus. Going to Bethlehem, he and St Paula there founded and became the first superiors of two monasteries, one for men and one for women, modelled on communities earlier established at the Mount of Olives by Rufinus of Aquileia and St Melania.

PILGRIMAGES

Thus East and West met in Palestine, and the "Holy Places" became one of the principal centres of early monasticism. The

Pilgrimages, whose popularity began at this time and continued even after the Arab invasion, had a double object: to see the land where Jesus had once dwelt and to visit the monasteries where his heroic modern disciples now lived. A contemporary of St Jerome, the virgin Etheria, who was a native of Gaul or Spain, has left a detailed description of her journey to Jerusalem and other holy places of the East in the early fourth century.

The beginning of the fifth century saw the appearance of more developed works on monasticism, such as the *Lausiac History of Palladius* (in Latin) and Cassian's *Conferences* (in Greek) in which the deeds and sayings of the holy abbots of Egypt or Palestine are recounted in an attractive and colourful style. These pages bring to life the Eastern monasticism which was now spread throughout Christendom and whose high ideal of asceticism and the spiritual life was to be a source of inspiration for centuries to come.

CHAPTER V

THE FATHERS OF THE CHURCH

Sanctity, whose most popular aspects we have just examined, was not the privilege of monks, after being that of the martyrs, for the greatest bishops, founders, administrators, preachers and theologians also attracted a spontaneous cultus. Most famous of these were the so-called Fathers of the Church whose writings were carefully treasured in the centuries to come as a rich store of spiritual and doctrinal nourishment. The names of these men (some of whom have earned the title of Doctor of the Church) dominate the period, and although they have already been mentioned in preceding chapters some more particular consideration. is called for.

THE EASTERN FATHERS

The first outstanding figure in the East is St Athanasius of Alexandria, the symbol of resistance to Arianism, the man of unyielding orthodoxy and of indomitable character who in the course of a long episcopate stood his ground against four successive emperors. Besides polemical pamphlets and treatises written in the heat of the Arian controversy he also composed many other works of an apologetic, exegetical or moral nature—not to speak of his life of St Antony which contributed so much to the popularity of monasticism. In the words of Mgr Duchesne: "By profession he was not a man of letters nor a scholar. Philosophical mysteries and academic problems he left to others: for his own purposes all he needed was a pen, paper, and the relevant documents." A forceful writer, he was above all a fearless and commanding man of action whose energy was chiefly responsible for the defeat of Arianism, and it was due to him that the see of Alexandria was able to play such an important rôle in the fourth and fifth centuries under his successors Theophilus (385–412) and Cyril (412–44). However, these prelates (of whom Cyril has left us many works of exegesis, theology and polemics) did not always defend such worthy causes. Nor were they as scrupulous in their methods, their campaigns against Chrysostom and Nestorius being more notable for ambition and cunning than for religious zeal.

Other Egyptian Fathers command greater respect, such as the lay theologian and teacher Didymus the Blind, abbot Serapion of Thmuis, called to the episcopate from a monastic cell, and abbot Isidore of Pelusium. In Palestine there were such figures as St Cyril of Jerusalem (348–86), author of some justly famed baptismal catecheses, and in Mesopotamia St Ephrem (306–73), the first theologian writing in Syriac and founder of the School of Nisibis, later moved to Edessa.

For the great names of the patristic age we must look to Cappadocia, in Asia Minor, the home of three men who together form an outstanding group of bishops: St Basil of Caesarea, his brother St Gregory of Nyssa, and their friend St Gregory of Nazianzus. All three came of Christian families and received an excellent literary training at Constantinople and at Athens, where one of their classmates was the future emperor Julian. This classical education left its mark on their style, which puts them in the rank of the best Greek authors. As religious writers, it is not difficult to understand the great reputation which they won in their lifetime and always retained.

St Basil, in Mgr Duchesne's words, "had every gift; an acknowledged personal holiness, a mind of fine cultivation, eloquence, deep understanding of the faith and an instinct for affairs." As metropolitan of Caesarea (370–79) he took a firm stand against the Arianizing emperor Valens, succeeded in restoring ecclesiastical communion between East and West after negotiations with Pope Damasus, and brought new penetration to dogmatic theology (particularly in his treatise on the divinity of the Holy Spirit). He too joined battle in the defence of ortho-doxy, but his activities as writer and pastor were not restricted to the limits of the Arian controversy. His monastic rules, which owed much to Eustathius of Sebaste, were widely propagated, and his sermons and letters touch on every aspect of the Christian religion; the *Address to Young Men* indicates how Christians may profit from pagan literature, and the homilies on the Crea-tion are at once a poetical exegesis of the first chapters of Genesis and a kind of *summa* of contemporary scientific knowledge. His bad health, a constant handicap, led to his early death before the age of fifty.

His younger brother Gregory, after the death of his wife, succeeded to the lesser episcopal see of Nyssa in Cappadocia which he held from 371 to 394. After some initial setbacks in the reign of Valens, his career was both less stormy and less con-spicuous than that of his elder brother and he hardly left his province except to take part in the great council of 381, at which he was entrusted with a mission in Arabia and chosen to deliver the funeral oration of the empress Flaccilla. His real fame is de-rived from his theological writings, the long treatises against the Arian Eunomius and against Apollinaris, the great *Catechetical Discourse* and his works of allegorical exegesis (after Origen) on the *Life of Moses* and the Song of Songs.

The friend Gregory, son of the bishop of Nazianzus in Cappa-docia, had a much more eventful and unsettled life. He was appointed by Basil to a newly created see in the rather dull provin-cial town of Sasima, but soon gave up his ministry and retired to monastic solitude in the Taurus Mountains. After the expulsion of the last Arian patriarch of Constantinople he was summoned as the successor, and soon became famous for his homilies to which the people flocked in crowds. But soon he tired of the tumult and wrangling of the capital and departed for the retire-ment of his native land where he was eventually compelled to settle down as bishop of Nazianzus. Unlike Basil or Athanasius he had no sense of pastoral vocation. His sensitive genius found its expression in meditation and in a many-sided literary composition which included sermons, letters and poems—true masterpieces which reflect the ardent, lofty spirit and susceptible, nervous character of their author. His spontaneity of ideas and brilliant literary gifts make him a very lively and appealing figure.

We find an equally attractive and ardent personality in a priest of Antioch who became patriarch of Constantinople, St John "of the Golden Mouth" or Chrysostom (354–407). Monk and finally bishop, at the end of his brief career, he was first and foremost a preacher who could sway whole crowds with his eloquence. In his fiery sermons he could given vent to unjust or tactless abuse (whether directed against the Jews of Antioch or the Empress of Constantinople) but he was nevertheless a master of Christian oratory, a powerful witness to Christological and sacramental doctrine, a commentator on Scripture (whose lessons he adapted for his contemporaries) and a champion of stern morality against every form of vice and foible. His courageous attempts at moral reform earned him the lasting hatred of clergy and Court alike: disgraced and exiled, he died a martyr to the cause of ecclesiastical liberty.

After Chrysostom, the Eastern Church produced no figures of comparable stature. We have some noteworthy but disputed theologians in the fifth century like Theodore of Mopsuestia in Cilicia and Theodoret of Cyrrhus in Syria, and in the following century some unoriginal exegetes like Procopius of Gaza, ascetical writers like Barsanuphius, John and Dorotheus of Gaza, and composers of verse hymns like Romanus the Melodist and his school, but none of these may be accounted a thinker or writer of real distinction. More eminent names were to appear in the seventh and eighth centuries. St Maximus the Confessor, who gave his life in the cause of orthodoxy, was an acute theologian and profound mystic, commentator and propagandist of the treatises attributed to Dionysius the Areopagite. St John Damascene, a monk at Jerusalem, was an eminent Doctor of the Church who championed the cult of images, the composer of liturgical hymns and author of many other works including a treatise on dogmatic theology which still remains a classic. His death marks the end of the patristic age in the East.

THE WESTERN FATHERS

In the West the patristic age, properly speaking, included only the authors of the imperial age of the fourth and fifth centuries. The Western counterpart of Athanasius during the Arian crisis was St Hilary, bishop of Poitiers from 350 to 367, a man of courage who also withstood the authoritarian claims of the Emperor Constantius II. Through him the Latin world was made aware of the subtle dangers of Arianism, and introduced to the principles of Trinitarian dogma and to the allegorical methods of Origenist exegesis. He is the first Western Doctor of the Church.

After him comes a Roman, St Ambrose of Milan—more a man of action than a thinker, more a pastor than a theologian. His treatises, sermons and letters range over a wide variety of religious themes but evince little originality: he uses Didymus the Blind for his proof of the divinity of the Holy Spirit, St Basil for his commentary on the six days of creation and even Cicero for a moral treatise. More important was the influence he wielded over successive emperors at Milan, directing them in the restoration of orthodoxy and the elimination of paganism. Gratian, Valentinian II and Theodosius all showed a submissiveness to the promptings of the Church and to the precepts of the Gospel which few later monarchs were to emulate.

The two other "giants" of the Western Church, St Jerome and St Augustine, stood outside the political arena. St Jerome, an Italian from Venetia, was a born fighter with a genius for combining extremes: a monk who spent long years in the world, an unwilling priest who exercised no ministry, a Westerner living mainly in the East, a scholar steeped in the classics who denied his Ciceronian training. His writings reveal two outstanding qualities: a formidable ability in controversy, which rises to great feeling in his defence of asceticism, and a profound knowledge of Scripture. He translated the Old Testament into Latin from the original Hebrew and edited a new version of the New Testament based on a collation of the best Greek manuscripts, completing this corpus of translations (our "Vulgate") by a series of learned commentaries.

Overshadowing the whole period is the powerful genius of St Augustine (354–430). Born in Africa and by profession a professor of rhetoric, he came to Christianity by way of Manicheism and neo-Platonism. After his conversion at Milan in 386 he returned to Africa where he was made priest, and later bishop of Hippo (395). No subsequent doctrinal controversy was complete without him: it was he who procured the decisive condemnation and hastened the downfall of Donatism, and he was also the first to deny the heresy of Pelagius. Above all, with his deeply philosophical spirit he could transcend every problem and prepare solutions that were sure and lasting: to everything he brought new penetration, whether it was the concept of the Church (in his controversies with the schismatics), Trinitarian dogma and moral theology (in his writing and preaching) or the interpretation of Scripture (in his commentaries on Genesis, the Psalms or the Gospels). Of his many achievements perhaps the greatest was his *City of God*, a meditation on the destiny of the Empire, written at the time of the first victorious barbarian onslaughts which led finally to the sack of Rome in 410. "Can Rome be eternal?" This was the question Augustine asked himself, and his answer was designed at once to refute pagan charges and to instruct the faithful. In his vision he sees two opposing cities: the earthly city, that is our present world where the good are mingled with the bad and where the godless prevail, and the heavenly city, which will be perfectly realized only in eternity but of which the Church here below is at once an image and a preparation. Transcending the superficial objections and superstitious fears of his contemporaries he transforms his contemplation into a whole philosophy of history, a treatise on the State and on the concept of peace. His influence on later thought, from the Middle Ages until recent times, has taken the form both of a philosophical Augustinism (a powerful influence on the Reformation and on Jansenism) and in a political Augustinism which asserts the Church's rights against the claims of the State.

On the eve of the great invasions, which he himself lived to see, St Augustine dominates every aspect of the world of Christian thought. A rapid and steep decline now developed, and darkness is enlightened only by the names of certain popes, more noted perhaps for their pastoral care than for their doctrine. St Leo the Great, who as pope (440–461) was faced with new invasions of Italy by Huns and Vandals, owes his title to his authoritative government of the Church and to the bold style and dogmatic precision which distinguish his letters and sermons and which are reflected in contemporary liturgical prayers. His death was followed by the collapse of the Empire in the West and the advent of barbarism. Yet by the time of St Gregory the Great, who reigned as pope from 590 to 604, Italy was once more under Byzantine rule and a part of the Christendom of the Empire, within which it represented the Roman tradition. Gregory, with his sense of the universality of the Church, saw beyond the newly traced boundaries of the Empire. His moral and liturgical writings link the Age of the Fathers, of whom he was the last, with the already dawning medieval epoch.

PART II

THE CHURCH AMONG THE BARBARIANS

The diversity we have already noted as a mark of the Church of the Empire, where a division was not long in appearing between East and West, was an even more pronounced feature of Christianity among the barbarians—those peoples who had remained outside the orbit of Roman rule, untouched by Greco-Latin civilization. In the East these "barbarians" were civilized, organized nations, and those nearest the Mediterranean were reached by Christianity from the third century onwards—in contrast with the more primitive Celtic and Germanic tribes of the West which were not evangelized until later. While dealing with the Roman Empire our terms of reference have been relatively uniform, but each of these main barbarian regions demands separate treatment, for the conditions accompanying the foundation and development of Christianity differed widely from one to another.

CHAPTER VI

THE FAR EAST

PERSIA

The most important of Rome's imperial neighbours, a country with whom she was nearly always at war, was Persia, heir to the kingdom of Parthia and mistress of an Empire which extended from Mesopotamia into the heart of Iran. Here the Sassanid dynasty, which reigned from the third to the seventh century, never wavered in its allegiance to the official pagan religion of the country, under the sway of a powerful hierarchical clergy (the *mobed* or magi): Christianity was regarded as an impious rival and (after its adoption by the Romans under Constantine) as the religion of the enemy. Yet there were Christians in Persia at a very early date—certainly in the region of Mesopotamia, which had a Semite population like the Roman provinces of Syria (Syriac has always been its ecclesiastical language). Though the origins of these communities are extremely obscure, they were certainly in existence at the time of Constantine, who in 336 addressed a letter to the Persian king, Sapor, on behalf of the Christians in that realm; and in 325 a Persian bishop was among the prelates attending the council of Nicaea. For the fourth century our information is limited to the persecution of Christians under Sapor II and Ardachir II: several bishops of Seleucia-Ctesiphon (the imperial capital) were arrested and put to death, to be followed by hundreds and soon thousands of the faithful. The massacres (whose brutal reality was embroidered in martyrologies composed by some of the survivors) lasted up to the end of the war with Rome in 384, when the cessation of hostilities brought a period of religious toleration. The see of Seleucia vacant for almost forty years, was filled once more and its bishop (the catholicos) acquired the position of primate or patriarch of the whole Persian Church. His authority over the five metropolitan sees established in the Western provinces was recognized at a national council held in 410, though in the East his subjects were more scattered.

The council of 410 enjoyed toleration and even support from the king, Yezdegerd I, who had officially proclaimed religious liberty. Relations between the Churches of the two rival Empires were again restored thanks to the good offices of Marutas, bishop of Martyropolis in Roman Mesopotamia. It was he who in 399 consecrated Isaac the Great as bishop of Seleucia and in 408 he returned on an official mission, bringing letters from the patriarch of Antioch which contained the Nicaean symbol and canons, hitherto not promulgated in Persia. Other Byzantine conciliar decrees were published at a second council of Seleucia in 420. Persian Christianity, now closely linked with the Churches of Syria, entered a period of remarkable vitality. However a fresh outbreak of persecution (420–22) under King Bahram V, instigated by the Mazdean clergy, resulted in the breaking off of relations with "the Western Fathers" (the bishops of the Roman Empire) at the council of Markabta. Later conciliar enactments (in 486 and 497) accentuated the schism even further, the marriage of clerics being not only authorized but enforced, and celibacy being permitted only for cloistered monks. In spite of this assertion of independence by the Persian Church, anxious to disassociate itself from the Roman enemy, there were further sporadic persecutions under Yezdegerd II and Peroz in the fifth century and under Chosroës in the sixth century. The many victims who suffered on these occasions were soon venerated as martyrs. Yet the Christians, never more than a minority in the country, henceforward enjoyed a considerable liberty and in practice Mazdeism was not strictly enforced according to the letter.

Marabba, the catholicos from 540 to 552, who as a convert from Mazdeism was legally liable to the death penalty, was freed and reprieved by king Chosroës after he had proved his loyalty in pacifying a southern revolt. With his energy and prestige,

Marabba also succeeded in restoring peace to the Church, putting an end to local schisms and disputes over a number of episcopal sees, and correcting certain abuses (concerning marriage within the degrees of affinity) and pagan superstitions.

After Marabba, the Persian kings often intervened in the nomination of the catholicos. The first royal choice, Joseph, who was a doctor by profession, antagonized all the bishops with his tyrannical caprices and was deposed by them in 567. Later nominations were more judicious: Ezechiel of Zabe, Ishoyabh of Arzun and Sabrisho of Lashom all proved themselves eminently worthy of the episcopate and presided over reforming councils.

However the schism with the Byzantine Churches entailed grave consequences for Persian Christianity. In the fourth century the Persian Church had remained immune to Arianism: the moralist Aphraates, of whom we have twenty-two homilies written in Syriac, shows a complete unawareness of the heresy. But in the fifth century the frontier no longer proved a barrier to doctrinal controversies. In 457 the School of Edessa, founded a hundred years earlier by St Ephrem, was expelled from Roman Mesopotamia by its Monophysite enemies, and this centre of Nestorianism now moved to Nisibis in the Sassanid Empire. The subsequent spread of Nestorianism was primarily due to Barsumas, the bishop of Nisibis, and to the catholicos Acacius. A council of Seleucia in 486 solemnly proclaimed Christ's two natures, divine and human, "without blending, mixture or confusion", and this definition now became the official doctrine of the Persian Church. In 585 it was confirmed by another council which denounced the opponents of Theodore of Mopsuestia and "those heretics who presume to attribute the properties and sufferings of Christ's human nature to the nature and hypostasis of the divine Word". Monophysite attempts at infiltration, led by Simeon of Beit Arsam in 497 and Ahudemmeh of Tagrit in 559, were doomed to failure and only the monks of Tur Abdin, following the trail of the caravans, obtained some successes in Adiabene (Assyria). The Nestorian monks under their leader and reformer Abraham of Kashtar in the sixth century waged an effective campaign against Monophysite propaganda and also against the teaching of Henana of Nisibis, a suspected Origenist who was in fact loyal to the orthodox definitions of Ephesus.

Christianity also reached Asia by way of the Mesopotamian trade-routes as they penetrated further East to the great commercial centres of India, to the isles of Socotora and Ceylon and to the shores of the Caspian, inhabited by Hephtalite Huns. The bishops of these far-flung countries all recognized the authority of the catholicos of Seleucia. All the Churches of Asia were to be overwhelmed by the tide of Islam in the seventh century, but long before this disaster their attachment to Nestorianism had cut them off from orthodox Christianity.

ARMENIA

The advent of Christianity to Armenia was swift and almost unopposed. The founder of the Church, Gregory the Illuminator, was an Armenian nobleman who was baptized and later consecrated bishop at Caesarea in Cappadocia. His first convert was the king Tiridates, and Christianity was established by royal authority as the religion of the State, Gregory becoming catholicos, or supreme head of the episcopate. This latter dignity was at first handed down from father to son since clerical celibacy was not observed. Indeed the religious framework remained that of the old traditional paganism: the new priesthood was recruited from the ranks of the old, the see of the catholicos was established at the former pagan shrine of Achtichat, the churches were simply converted temples (which retained many of their original trappings), and the morals of people and clergy do not appear to have undergone any notable change. The monarchy regarded the new religion perhaps as a means of countering the Mazdeism of their Persian enemies and (after Constantine's conversion) as an opportunity of forging closer links with their Roman allies. A more lasting and spontaneous movement of conversion came later.

The first of the reformers was Nerses, catholicos from 364 to 374, who, like Gregory (his great-great-grandfather), had been educated in Roman Cappadocia. He promulgated disciplinary

canons enacted at the first council of Achtichat and founded
monasteries, schools and charitable institutions, castigating the
immoralities of the Court and finally falling victim to the king's
harshness. After a renewal of bickering and conflict, the lead was
eventually taken by his son Sahak the Great, who became catholicos in 390 or 402. Not long before his accession Armenia had
been divided up according to a treaty between Theodosius and
the Persian king by which the western half of the country was in-
corporated into the Byzantine Empire, and the remaining four-
fifths became a protectorate of the Persians, who suppressed the
Armenian monarchy and in 428 annexed the country completely.
Inevitably the new régime came into conflict with the episcopate:
Sahak was deposed by the Persian overlords who for many years
appointed a catholicos of their own choice. But when Yezdegerd
attempted to impose Mazdeism on the country in 450, the people
resisted stoutly and with such success that religious liberty was
eventually granted by King Peroz. Moreover, the Church gained
new vigour from the persecution. At the beginning of the century
Sahak had inspired a new religious movement based on a closer
study of Scripture, and later the monk Machtots (or Mesrob)
originated the first written form of the Armenian language, with
his invention of an alphabet of thirty-six letters similar to Greek
characters. Due to his initiative, translations of the Bible and of
Greek and Syrian Fathers were commissioned and the first
Armenian literature came into being.

At first the Armenian Christians had looked for guidance to
their mother Church of Caesarea in Cappadocia, but the reformers of the fifth century turned instead for their intellectual
training and doctrinal example to Constantinople. The disturb-
ances following the annexation in 428 had prevented the Armenian bishops from attending the council of Ephesus but in 435
the pressure of Nestorian propaganda from Syria led the council
of Achtichat to seek direction from Proclus, Patriarch of Constantinople, who sent back a treatise clearly stating the dogma of
the Incarnation. A later council, held at Chahapivan in 444, condemned the Messalians—a sect not unlike the Spanish Priscillianists, who while vowing themselves to absolute poverty and to

prayer, rejected the Church's authority, replacing her doctrine with an angelology and a demonology of their own making.

Armenia, however, was soon swept into the Monophysite current and became separated from the Byzantine Church. The persecution of Yezdegerd had prevented the Armenians from attending Chalcedon, and they only resumed contact with the Church of the Empire at a time when Zeno and Anastasius were enforcing throughout their territories acceptance of the *Henoticon* and the break with Rome. In 491 the definitions of Chalcedon were solemnly repudiated at a council held in Valarshapat (the new see of the catholicos), and this condemnation was repeated at the two councils of Dvin in 506 and 554. It was not difficult for Monophysite controversies to represent the Fathers of Chalcedon as Nestorians, since the vital concepts of nature, person, and hypostatic union were distorted in Armenian translations of the original Greek definitions. The schism also spread to the neighbouring kingdoms of Transcaucasia, Iberia (Georgia) and Aghuania (Albania), which had evidently been converted soon after Armenia; the catholicos of Aghuania attended the councils of Valarshapat and Dvin but was later prevailed upon by the patriarch of Jerusalem to maintain his loyalty to Roman orthodoxy. For a while Armenia returned to the orthodox fold under Heraclius, who called a special council at Erzerum in 632, but the reunion was clumsily imposed and opposition to Chalcedon remained deeply ingrained. Constans II could not prevent the return of the schism, which was reintroduced by the catholicos Nerses after the council of Dvin in 650.

This bitter conflict between Byzantium and Armenia greatly assisted the Arabs, who after varying successes eventually became masters of the country in 660. Under the Caliphate the Armenians remained as steadfastly Monophysite as the Persians remained steadfastly Nestorian. Even after the Byzantine reconquest all hope of reconciliation was frustrated by the Greek refusal to tolerate local customs, exemplified by the condemnation of Armenian liturgical and disciplinary peculiarities at the council of Constantinople (692). After the council of Mantzikert in 719 the Armenian schism became final and irrevocable.

ABYSSINIA

At the southern extremity of the oriental world, Christianity had penetrated the African kingdom of Axum (modern Abyssinia) in the middle of the fourth century, under Constantius. According to tradition, the first apostle of the country was Frumentius, a young man shipwrecked on its shores, who remained to baptize the original native population, including their king Ezana, and who later received episcopal consecration at the hands of St Athanasius in Alexandria. No more is known then until the end of the fifth century, when the conversion of king Andas brought over almost the whole country to Christianity. To this period also may be dated the arrival of the "nine saints" (still venerated in the Abyssinian Church), a group of monks— probably of Syrian origin—who popularized Christian asceticism and translated the Gospels into the Ge'ez language. By the time of Justinian, with whom the Axumite king Ella Atsbéha was connected by alliance, the "abuna" who presided over the Abyssinian Church was regularly consecrated by the patriarch of Alexandria. This close link with the Coptic Church and the formative influence of Syrian monks gave Abyssinian Christianity that exclusively Monophysite character which it still bears today.

ARABIA

The first apostle of the Himyarite (or Homerite) kingdom of Yemen which maintained close relations with Axum, across the Red Sea, was the monk Theophilus, who is traditionally supposed to have been sent in the fourth century by the emperor Constantius and who is credited with the building of a church at Safar, the capital, and with the conversion of the Yemenite king. But this mission, if it be authentic, was not lasting and there is no historical evidence of widespread conversion until the beginning of the sixth century, when churches were established on the coast at Safar and Aden, and inland at Nedjran. The country was then a dominion of the Christian king of Axum, but later a national revolt led by the Arab chieftain Dhû Nuwâs, a convert to Judaism, led to a violent outbreak of persecution: in 523 the Christians of Safar and Nedjran were brutally massacred and their churches turned into synagogues. Christianity was only restored by force when the rebellion was crushed by the king of Axum. Shortly afterwards the Axumite viceroy Sumaïfa (Esimphaios) was defeated by a native Christian chieftain, Abraha. Under Abraha and his son (roughly from 530 to 570) the Church remained at peace till the conquest of Yemen by the Persians.

The northern region of Arabia, closer to the Roman province of Syria, was evangelized at an early date and a number of nomad chieftains were converted along with their tribes in the fourth and fifth centuries. Among them were queen Maouvia, baptized by the monk-bishop Moses, king Obadiah, baptized by a hermit also called Moses, and the phylarchs Zocomos and Aspebet (of whom the latter was to become a bishop himself). All these tribes on the imperial frontier were later collected into a vast principality which Justinian put under the authority of Harith the Ghassanid, a fanatical adherent of Syrian Monophysitism who reigned from 530 to 570. At his request a bishop, consecrated by the patriarch of Alexandria, was sent by the empress Theodora in 542 and numerous monasteries were founded along the desert caravan-trails. This bishopric survived the break-up of the Ghassanid kingdom in 585 and lasted a few more years until the Persian conquest.

The Lakhmid kingdom, on the borders of Arabia and Sassanid Mesopotamia, always remained a protectorate of the Persian Empire. Thus the see founded in the fifth century at Hira, the Lakhmid capital, was always Nestorian in its allegiance and dependent upon the catholicos of Seleucia.

All these Semitic peoples, naturally attracted to mysticism by their racial temperament or by the influence of the desert, had a great veneration for ascetics and anchorites (the Arabs of Hira flocked over the Roman frontier in crowds to gaze at Simon the Stylite on his pillar) and the propagation of the faith in these Arab lands was very largely the work of monks.

However, in the remoter corners of the Roman and Persian provinces and of the Yemenite kingdom, the Gospel first came in the train of merchants, along the caravan trails. Long before Mohammed, the shrine of the Kaaba at Mecca was drawing pilgrims from Abyssinia, the Yemen and Syria. And though there was no organized Church among the Qoraïchites, there was certainly a number of Jews and Christians like Waraqa, who was known to Mohammed—a fact which may explain the Jewish and Christian influence which is discernible in his doctrinal system. This indubitable kinship did not prevent Islam from becoming the Church's most violent foe, and during the seventh and eighth centuries the sweeping victories of Arab armies from Egypt to Spain on one side and to Persia on the other were to deal Eastern and even Western Christianity a catastrophic blow.

CHAPTER VII

THE CELTIC LANDS

Though Gaul and Britain were both Celtic, by "the Celtic lands" we mean primarily those countries which lay outside the orbit of imperial power and in which the native Celtic populations preserved their independence—the West and North of Britain, the island of Hibernia or Scottia (Ireland) and (from the fifth century onwards) Brittany.

Very little is known about Christianity in Roman Britain. Several bishoprics existed there in the fourth century, and in important matters the Churches of Gaul seem to have exercised a decisive influence, whether it was in importing (and later resisting) Arianism or in stamping out the heresy of the Briton Pelagius. Victricius of Rouen and Germanus of Auxerre crossed the Channel several times on special missions—though we possess little information about the disputes they came to settle. These remote lands also engaged the attention of the papacy. In 429 Pope Celestine authorized the mission of Germanus of Auxerre, and in 431 he sent out the missionary Bishop Palladius to bring the Gospel to Ireland—the "barbarian isle". After they had been finally cut off from the Empire in 442 the Celtic Churches became more isolated, leading an independent life of their own. Our first historical records also begin at this period, which saw the evangelization of Ireland by the British missionary Patrick (432–61) and the emigration of British Christians to the mainland of France (*c.* 460).

BRITTANY

Little is known about the first immigrant settlers. The invasion of the pagan Anglo-Saxons which put an end to Roman rule in Britain put the native Britons to flight, and while some took refuge in Cornwall or in the mountains of Wales, others crossed the sea to settle in the north-western peninsula of Gaul—thereafter known as Brittany. The movement began in the middle of the fifth century, for we find a "bishop of the Bretons" attending the council of Tours in 461, and was continued well into the sixth century. With the immigrants, who crossed from Cornwall in large groups, came their religious leaders. Though some of these, like St Corentin, St Samson, St Malo and St Guénolé, were later venerated as apostles they were not like missionaries entering a pagan land, for Brittany already possessed three bishoprics at Nantes, Rennes and Vannes, which continued to exist alongside the new sees established by the settlers (Quimper, Trécor, Dol, Alet, Saint-Pol-de-Léon and Saint Brieuc—the last two named after their respective founders). The new bishops refused to recognize the authority of the metropolitan of Tours, and disregarded his directives on liturgical procedure in 515 and the decree about episcopal consecrations passed at the provincial council of 567. Separated as they were by differences of language and customs, natives and settlers long maintained a bitter antagonism.

CORNWALL AND WALES

Even less is known about the British Churches of Cornwall and Wales—that is, if we rule out the prodigious and fantastic legends so beloved of Celtic hagiographers. Welsh Christianity was centred on the great monasteries which arose between the fifth and seventh centuries: Llantwit, whose founder Illtyd had been ordained priest by St Germanus of Auxerre, Menevia and Llan Carvan, founded by St David and St Cadoc, and finally Bangor Is-Coed with its famous abbot Deiniol and its population of more than two thousand monks. Tradition has it that these monks were massacred after an Anglo-Saxon victory, falling with the Welsh warriors whom they had supported in battle by fasting and prayer. Here also the animosity between the two races was such that the Celts even refused to evangelize the pagan conquerors. The Picts of barbarian Galloway on the Scottish border received the Gospel at the beginning of the fifth century from St Ninian, a missionary trained in Rome, but their conversion seems to have been short-lived. The Anglo-Saxons in their turn were to be converted from Rome, and also from Ireland, whose Church soon showed its missionary genius.

IRELAND

The conversion of Ireland, begun by the Roman missionary Palladius, is chiefly associated with the name of Patrick, who crossed to the island from Britain after a period spent in Gaul at Lérins and Auxerre. His earlier captivity in the country had given him a knowledge of the Irish language and he worked tirelessly among the people for thirty-three years, converting the tribal chieftains, overthrowing the power of the Druids and founding the first churches—notably that of Armagh, which later became the primatial see of all Ireland. The mystical fervour so characteristic of the people soon produced an abundance of monastic vocations, and the rural nature of society in a country always ravaged by clan warfare led to the establishment of non-urban monastic bishoprics. In Ireland the monastery took the place of the continental *civitas*, and its abbot was at the same time bishop of the surrounding territory. Each of these monasteries (all dating from the sixth century) venerated its own founder saint: St Enda at Killean, on an island off the west coast, St Finnian at Clonard, in the east, another Finnian at Moville in Ulster, St Kieran at Clonmacnois on the Shannon, St Kevin at Glendalough, St Brendan at Clonfert and St Comgall at Bangor in Ulster. If we are to believe certain traditions, each of these foundations contained several thousand monks, not counting a vast multitude of hermits. Certainly, cenobites greatly outnumbered the secular clergy.

Our information about these monastic communities is mainly derived from their so-called Rules, which are not so much ordered codes of legislation as expressions of ascetical teaching or lists of customs and observances. The life of the monks was divided between prayer, study and manual labour, and their liturgy was centred round the recitation of the psalter which they performed with arms outstretched or with prostrations and genuflexions. There were also other mortifications of a fiercer kind, such as immersion in rivers or pools during winter or prolonged and rigorous fasts (far more exacting in the Irish climate than in the eastern deserts). The monasteries themselves were very simply constructed, like pioneer settlements with their separate huts of wood or dry stones, enclosed by a rough palisade. The eremitical life too had many devotees, and the rocky coves of the Irish coastline offered many lonely refuges for those who sought solitude and contemplation.

Monasticism, therefore, was an essential feature of the Irish Church and of Celtic Christianity as a whole. In Wales and Brittany alike the chief authority was in the hands of the abbot-bishops, and the monastery and episcopal see (Breton *lann*) often became synonymous. It was by the spread of monastic observances that the practice of private confession and later the use of "penitentials" (lists of sins with their corresponding penances) became established among the laity.

The Celtic Church also maintained other idiosyncrasies such as their method of reckoning the date of Easter. The origins of this deviation are difficult to trace, but it is conjectured that the British system was identical with an earlier reckoning universally observed at the beginning of the fourth century, which had subsequently been replaced at Rome by the system of Victorius of Aquitaine in the fifth century and by that of Dionysius Exiguus in the sixth. Celtic ignorance of these later changes may be explained by the isolation which followed the Anglo-Saxon invasions, and they were confirmed in their nonconformity by a deep-rooted xenophobia. One part of Ireland adopted the Roman reckoning in the seventh century but the Churches of the north, and those of Scotland, Wales and Cornwall held out till the eighth century. Similarly the Celtic tonsure long differed from the continental form, and their episcopal consecrations were commonly performed by one prelate instead of three. Before these variations could be reconciled there were many sharp conflicts, especially after the beginning of the seventh century when the monks and clergy of Britain or Ireland came into contact with the outside world.

THE CELTIC EXPANSION

These Irishmen soon proved to be great travellers, inspired by the ideal of becoming "Christ's voyagers" and of spreading far and wide their true missionary apostolate. The evangelization of Iceland in the eighth century is not historically guaranteed, but the expeditions of St Cormac to the Orkneys and of St Columba to Scotland (in the middle of the sixth century) are beyond doubt. St Columba had already founded several monasteries in the north of Ireland before he resolved to join his fellow-countrymen who had emigrated to northernmost Britain (which now appropriated Ireland's old name of Scottia). Here he converted the native Picts to Christianity and founded many monasteries, most famous of which was Iona in the Western Isles. From this "mother-house" at Iona set forth the apostles of the Saxon kingdom of Northumbria, St Aidan, St Finan and St Colman, all bishops of Lindisfarne off the North Sea coast.

Not long after Columba's departure for Scotland, his near-namesake St Columbanus set out for the Continent, to become the founder of monasteries in Gaul: first, the Burgundian houses of Luxueil and Fontaines and later Faremoutiers and Jouarre near Meaux (of which one of his disciples became bishop). Some of his companions established other centres of Irish monasticism: St Kilian near Arras, St Gall by the Lake of Constance (where his great foundation bears his name), and later St Fursey at Péronne, St Rombaut at Malines, St Livin at Ghent, St Virgil at Salzburg and others besides. There may have been some impostors or eccentrics among these wanderers, and certainly the Irish customs (ranging from the tonsure to the Easter reckoning) caused scandal and conflict, but this does not diminish the momentous importance of the Celtic monastic expansion in the history of European Christianity. Though they came to the Roman world as strangers, the Irish monks were familiar with Latin which they used together with the Irish language in their liturgy and sacred sciences, and this bilingualism enabled them to overcome any provinciality of outlook and to share in the intellectual life of the Latin world. Ireland, not long before known as the "Barbarian Isle", was now the "Isle of Saints", and its flourishing Christianity provides a striking contrast with the decline of the old Churches of the continent, now experiencing the Germanic conquests.

CHAPTER VIII

THE GERMANIC KINGDOMS

In the fifth century Roman authority throughout the Western Empire had been steadily submerged beneath the waves of on-coming Germanic invaders, and the old Roman provinces fell into the hands of new masters, Visigoths and Ostrogoths, Vandals, Suevians, Burgundians, Alemans, Franks, Angles and Saxons, and later the Lombards. Most of these Barbarians had already come into contact with Christianity, except for Attila's Huns—Mongols whose invasion was like an endless hurricane of terror. A "bishop of the Goths", that is the Ostrogoths settled in the Crimea, was present at the Council of Nicaea, and later the mission of Ulfila brought the Gospel to the Visigothic peoples on the left bank of the lower Danube. Ulfila, himself a Visigoth, received his training in the Empire and was consecrated bishop in 341 by Eusebius of Nicomedia. On his return he preached Christianity in the Arian form he had encountered among the Romans, and he also created the first Gothic literature with his translation of the Gospels. However, not all the Goths were Arians, for certain bishops are known to have been loyal to Nicaea, while some belonged to a sect of Audians, which had re-fused to accept the Nicaean ruling on the date of Easter. Other barbarian peoples had been converted to Catholicism, like the Marcomans under Queen Frigitil (c. 396), the Huns evangelized by Niceta of Remesiana and Theotimus of Tomi, and the Burgundians on the banks of the Rhine (both before 430), but these results were not lasting. Of the Germanic tribes who took over the Empire *en masse* later in the fifth century, nearly all were Arians.

THE ARIAN KINGDOMS

Africa

This religious conflict between Barbarian heresy and Roman orthodoxy certainly contributed to the hostility which divided the native inhabitants of the Empire from the Germanic invaders who settled in the provinces of Gaul, Spain and Africa during the fifth century. The newcomers were not only hated as devastators but resented as heretics, and their individual peculiarities of doctrine and liturgical practice helped to estrange them still further from Roman traditions.

In the first independent barbarian kingdom, established by the Vandals in Africa, these differences developed into violent conflict. Ten years after his first landing, the Vandal king Genseric established his capital at Carthage in 439 and a savage persecution ensued, later continued by his son Huneric. The clergy suffered banishment or execution, the churches were destroyed or taken over by the Arians, and all officials were obliged to adopt the State religion established by the new régime. A phantom conference between the bishops of both sides in 484 seemed to mark the utter collapse of Catholicism in Vandal Africa. But the persecution, described in the impassioned narrative of Victor of Vita, was not always enforced with the same pressure, and the abatement under king Gontamund (487) and under his successor Thrasamund allowed the Church to reorganize her forces. Polemical treatises against Arianism were composed by Vigilius, bishop of Thaspe, and by Fulgentius of Ruspe who had been deported to Sardinia. Yet the large number of apostasies made it necessary for Pope Felix (487) and Pope Agapitus (535) to state the conditions required for readmission of the lapsed, whether clerics or laymen. Catholics were eventually granted their liberty under Hilderic, the last Vandal king, shortly before Justinian's triumphal conquest of Africa (534).

Gaul and Spain

In Europe the Germanic conquerors showed greater toleration. After the collapse of the western Empire in 476, Gaul and

Spain were divided up between the three separate nations of Visigoths, Suevians, and Burgundians. Of these the Burgundians, along the Saône and in the Rhône valley near Lyons, were part Arian and part Catholic, with an Arian monarchy. At length St Avitus, bishop of Vienne, succeeded in converting king Gondebald, or at least his son Sigismund who succeeded in 516, and it was not long before the people followed their ruler's example.

The first king of the Suevians, in the north-western region of Spain, was a Catholic, but his successor Remismund adopted Arianism in 466. Due to the influence of the Pannonian monk Martin of Braga, the dynasty returned to Catholic orthodoxy a century later (563) under King Theodomir, followed by his whole people.

The Visigoths were still more tenacious in their Arian loyalties, and a campaign of persecution was waged by their first independent sovereign, Euric (466–84), whose empire extended from the Loire down to Cadiz and took in the Mediterranean coasts from the Rhône to the Straits of Gibraltar. In Gaul a considerable number of bishops was deposed about 475 for their opposition to the Gothic régime (among them Sidonius Apollinaris at Clermont) and the sees were left unfilled. In 505 King Alaric II took similar measures against Caesarius of Arles and several bishops in Aquitaine. But the loss of their provinces in Gaul, which had been antagonized by the persecutions and fell into Frankish hands, taught the Visigothic rulers a lesson. In Spain the Catholics were now granted wide liberties, manifested in the holding of councils and the re-establishment of regular relations with the papacy. This was the age of St Leander of Seville, whose apostolic labours were crowned by the conversion of the sons of King Leovigild. The elder, Hermenegild, was put to death for rebellion against his father, but his younger brother Recared brought the whole Visigothic nation over to Catholicism on his accession to the throne in 585.

Italy

Meanwhile the other great branch of the Gothic family, the Ostrogoths, had settled in Italy. Their leader Theodoric the Great

(491–526), who was officially at least the legitimate viceroy of the Emperor, showed a scrupulous respect for the senatorial system and traditions of Rome and adopted a policy of great liberality towards his Catholic subjects, particularly with regard to the Holy See. His relations with Pope Gelasius were excellent and the attitude at the time of the schism between Symmachus and the anti-pope Lawrence (498–502) was circumspect and in general conducive to the independence of the Church. Similarly, after the Ostrogothic annexation of Provence, when Caesarius of Arles was accused of treason towards the new régime, Theodoric magnanimously set him at liberty. Only at the end of his reign was he driven by the opposition of a group of Roman aristocrats (which included the philosopher Boethius) to take harsher measures against the Catholics: Pope John I was sent on an embassy to the Court of Constantinople and died of brutal treatment soon after his return (526) and his successor Felix IV was imposed as the royal nominee. After Theodoric his daughter Amalasuntha was liberal in her policy towards the "Romans", but the Gothic aristocracy regarded Catholics and Byzantines alike with the same hostility. Hence the Holy See became inescapably involved in the long conflict which set succeeding Gothic generals, Theodatus, Witiges and Totila, against the armies of Justinian. After the death of Pope Agapitus at Constantinople where he had been sent for negotiations (536) the Goths imposed their own candidate Silverius, who was in his turn deposed and replaced in 537 after the Byzantine victory. After many grievous trials the Ostrogoths were finally driven out of Rome and Italy in 552, but the terrible struggle had left the Church and the whole country cruelly stricken and maimed.

Nor was this the end, for soon afterwards the land was again overwhelmed by a new wave of barbarian invaders, the Arian Lombards. By the end of the sixth century they had taken over from the Empire the whole of the Po valley plain and a tract of peninsular Italy—excluding the exarchate of Ravenna to the east and the duchy of Rome to the west, which were not added till the eighth century. Their warlike raids and their brutality were the cause of further suffering throughout Italy. Half the episcopal sees were eliminated in the havoc and at Rome the pope had to pay tribute to the Lombard king in order to save the city, even though the Church's property had already been confiscated. Yet there was no systematic persecution. The barbarism of the Lombards presented a greater menace than their heresy and as the people gradually became more civilized (to the extent of exchanging their Germanic language for Latin) so Catholicism made progress. A Catholic queen, the Bavarian princess Theodelinda, ruled in the name of her infant son at the beginning of the seventh century, and though her immediate successors were Arians the dynasty was finally converted to Catholicism under Aribert (652–662) and his son Perctarit (671–688).

In this age of turmoil, when Italy was the battleground of Ostrogoths and Byzantines and then Byzantines and Lombards, many found refuge and security in the Church. Before the middle of the sixth century Cassiodorus, a former minister of Theodoric, founded the monastery of Vivarium on his estates in Bruttium, where he wrote his *Historia Ecclesiastica Tripartita* and several manuals which were destined to become the text-books of medieval instruction in the "liberal arts", and where he collected his unique library of the classics of Latin literature. Earlier still St Benedict had founded monasteries at Subiaco and Monte Cassino which he provided with his own rule. Though Vivarium does not seem to have survived its founder, it handed on a precious intellectual tradition to Benedictine monachism which had originally devoted itself exclusively to manual labour. The figures of St Benedict and of St Gregory the Great, the pope (590–604) who founded a Benedictine monastery at Rome and fought the evils of the day with tireless energy, foreshadow an approaching revival.

THE VISIGOTHIC THEOCRACY

The Arian kingdoms were all short-lived, and those which were converted to Catholicism had no opportunity to develop a new, appropriate policy. The Catholic reign of Hilderic among the Vandals was a prelude to the Byzantine conquest (534), while the conversion of Sigismund and Theodomir, of the Burgundians and Suevians respectively, were closely followed by the Frankish and Visigothic invasions (534 and 585). The Visigoths alone maintained their Spanish dominions for more than a century after their conversion to orthodoxy, and their unique experiment in Catholic monarchy deserves special mention.

The vitality of the Spanish Church during this period may be attributed largely to the work of an outstanding group of bishops, all monastically trained, and all authors of theological, moral and literary treatises: Leander of Seville, his brother and successor Isidore, and the bishops of Toledo, Eugenius, Ildefonsus and Julian. The most notable of these was Isidore of Seville (560–636), who has been called the last of the Fathers, by reason of his encyclopedic work, a kind of *summa* of sacred and profane sciences which to some extent completes the intellectual achievement of antiquity.

But the distinguishing feature of seventh-century Spanish Catholicism was a close union between Church and State amounting even to caesaropapism. The kings, who were solemnly anointed at their accession, directed ecclesiastical affairs with a firm hand, claiming the right of appointing bishops and convoking councils, in which they took a personal part. Even the papacy, which now seldom intervened in Spanish affairs, recognized this practice for in 682 we find Pope Leo II requesting the Visigothic king to make known to the Spanish bishops the condemnation of Monothelism and to ensure their assent. But the term theocracy is equally appropriate, since the influence of State over Church was reciprocal. In a régime where the monarchy was elective and often disputed, the bishops had a major part to play in controlling the succession and the sovereign's freedom of action, often asserting their authority on moral issues or to safeguard the common good.

In this context, St Isidore reaffirmed St Ambrose's teaching on the duties of a Christian prince. So too the series of councils at Toledo legislated for civil society as well as for the Church, and the new Code approved by the bishops provided the nation with a common law (racial integration had followed closely on the union of the Churches). Toledo itself, previously the political capital, now became also the primatial see with authority over the other five metropolitans and eighty bishops of the kingdom, which included the province of Narbonne north of the Pyrenees. The council of 589 which crushed Arianism in Spain was followed by many others, and their innumerable decrees give us a clear and detailed picture of the Visigothic Church. Provincial synods were to supervise the carrying out of the general conciliar decisions and to check the conduct of civil officials, while the bishops superintended the education of their clergy, the maintenance of discipline, the establishment of rural parishes and the observance of the national (Mozarabic) liturgy.

This close union between Church and State gave Spanish Catholicism an unrivalled vitality. After fresh condemnations of Priscillianism and the official rejection of Arianism the exstirpation of heresy was complete, and the country was impervious to the theological controversies of the East, even after Justinian's establishment of a Byzantine province in Southern Spain. Moreover there was a gradual disappearance of pagan superstition, vigorously combated in the country districts by St Martin of Braga. The Jews remained the only dissenters but their numerous communities were gravely weakened in the harsh persecution inflicted by king Sisebut. In spite of protest from Isidore of Seville, championing liberty of conscience, they were forced to choose between conversion and exile. The persecution only succeeded in producing unbelieving Christians and resentful exiles, and the fierce hatred which it engendered in its Jewish victims was one of the reasons for the sudden Visigothic collapse under the Arab onslaught in 711.

THE ANGLO-SAXON CHURCH

Of all the Germanic peoples who invaded Roman territory, only two were pagan or remained pagan for any length of time— the Anglo-Saxons and the Franks who settled in Britain and northern Gaul, farthest outposts of the Empire.

The Anglo-Saxon landings on the coasts of the Channel and

North Sea began in the early fifth century. There was no racial assimilation, for the native Celts were driven westward and, as we have seen, scorned any attempt to convert the hated invaders. By the end of the sixth century the Jutes, Angles and Saxons were firmly installed in their seven kingdoms, all pagan. There was a bishop from Gaul at the Kentish Court as chaplain to Queen Bertha, a Frankish Catholic princess, but he undertook no apostolate and there was no real mission until the arrival of the Benedictine monk Augustine, sent from Rome on the initiative of Gregory the Great. King Ethelbert of Kent, who as the husband of Bertha was already well-disposed, gave the Roman envoys a warm welcome and soon received baptism together with several thousands of the Jutes (597). Augustine became the first bishop of the country, with his see at Canterbury, the Kentish capital, and he consecrated two of his companions as bishops of London and Rochester. Even as early as this the pope provided for the creation of two metropolitan sees and twenty-four dioceses and sent his emissary detailed and prudent instructions on the methods he was to adopt for his mission: the transition was to be effected gradually, and the customs and shrines of the pagans were to be respected and simply adapted to the new faith. The effects of this policy were seen in the swift progress of Christianity among the various Anglo-Saxon kingdoms. Kent offered the least resistance, in spite of some temporary opposition from King Ethelbert's son and successor Edbald, and Essex also followed after some vicissitudes; in East Anglia King Redwald reverted to paganism after submitting to baptism, but the new faith became solidly established under his sons; in Northumbria King Edwin together with his nobles and even the pagan priests received baptism in 627 at the hands of the Roman monk Paulinus, who became the first bishop of York and converted this entire Angle nation of the North. Later, Northumbrian Christianity suffered some setbacks, but the reign of Oswald, the founder of a new dynasty, who had been converted at Iona, saw the introduction of Celtic missionaries who founded the bishopric of Lindisfarne. Oswald was also responsible for the conversion of the King of Wessex (c. 640), who founded the bishoprics of Dorchester and

Winchester. Finally the Gospel penetrated to the two kingdoms of Mercia and Sussex.

By 680 the Anglo-Saxon Church was already flourishing, and a native clergy had taken the place of the original Roman or Irish missionaries. The most famous of its churchmen is Wilfrid (634–710), a monk who received his training at Lindisfarne, and later at Lyons and Rome. As abbot of the monastery of Ripon near York, Wilfrid played a decisive rôle at the conference of Whitby (664) where King Oswy of Northumbria declared for the Roman, as against the Celtic, reckoning of Easter. After becoming bishop of York he worked for a time in association with Theodore of Canterbury (a Greek monk who had been appointed to the primatial see by Pope Vitalian at the request of the King of Kent) but his taste for liturgical pomp and his ambition to make York an independent metropolitan see brought him under suspicion with the primate and with Egfrid, the new king of Northumbria, who removed him from the see of York (678) and defied a papal ruling in Wilfrid's favour. Reinstated by Egfrid's successor in 686, he was soon exiled again and appealed once more to Rome, eventually spending the last years of his stormy career as bishop of Lichfield and then of Hexham. Another notable figure of Northumbrian monasticism was Benet Biscop (628–690) who travelled to Rome with Wilfrid; returning with Theodore he became abbot of the monastery of Saints Peter and Paul at Canterbury, and later after more journeys to Rome founded other monasteries in Northumbria. These close and frequent communications with the Roman Church gave England her liturgy, her ecclesiastical discipline, her monastic legislation, her artistic traditions and intellectual life. Gregorian chant was introduced by Benet Biscop, while the construction of stone churches was started by Wilfrid with the help of masons and craftsmen from Gaul and Italy; these English churches seem to have been the first with glass windows, made necessary by the climate. Monastic schools taught Latin and even Greek, besides producing liturgical compositions and copies of the pagan classics, for the Anglo-Saxon scriptoria have left us Missals, Sacramentaries and manuscripts of every kind which reveal an exquisite perfection of calligraphy and miniature-work. This highly developed culture found expression in the eighth century in the writings of the Venerable Bede, great scholar and author of numerous Latin works on grammar, prosody, exegesis and theology—in addition to some poetry and several English versions of Scripture. Besides his Latin, he knew Greek and even a little Hebrew. A follower of Bede was Egbert, bishop of York from 732 to 766, author of a Pontifical and a Penitential, and founder of the famous School of York which was to be so influential in the Carolingian Empire.

The thriving and vigorous state of the Anglo-Saxon and Irish Churches in the seventh and eighth centuries was indeed an example to Continental Christianity.

FRANKISH CATHOLICISM

The Franks were converted much earlier than the Anglo-Saxon tribes and under very different conditions, although in both cases a decisive rôle was played by the monarchy. The original inhabitants of Gaul had been left undisturbed by the Frankish invasion and continued to form the majority of the population, so that the old Gallo-Roman Christianity still survived without substantial alteration except in the north, where the native Belgic people had virtually been supplanted by the Franks: this region north of the line Boulogne-Bavai-Cologne (which today still marks the linguistic boundary between French and Flemish), and the Rhineland overrun by Alemans and Ripuarian Franks, both became pagan after the middle of the fifth century and lost all their bishoprics. The Salian Franks first settled round the mouths of the Meuse and Escaut, with their capital at Tournai, but in 486 their king Clovis established his Court at Soissons or Rheims, occupying the whole Parisian region as far as the boundaries of the Burgundian and Visigothic kingdoms. Clovis was a pagan but the influence of two Christians soon made itself felt on his life: that of Remigius (Remi), bishop of Auxerre, who exhorted the young king to justice and reverence for the bishops, and that of Clotilde, the Burgundian Catholic princess who became his queen in 501. These influences soon led to his conversion, and after his

victory over the Alemans at Tolbiac he publicly acknowledged
"the God of Clotilde", receiving baptism at Rheims in 506 (more
probably than in 496, as usually stated). This profession of
Catholicism, in which Clovis was followed as a matter of course
by the mass of his people, made a considerable impression in the
Arian kingdoms of Gaul. Without compromising his loyalty to
his Burgundian sovereign, Avitus the bishop of Vienne made the
significant gesture of sending the new convert his congratula-
tions, while many bishops of the persecuted Visigothic Church
found their awakened interest interpreted as treason. Thus the
way was already prepared for the Frankish armies who marched
into the Visigothic provinces in 507. The victorious Clovis was
hailed as a liberator throughout the south-west, and on his return
he gave proof of his Catholic devotion at the tomb of St Martin
in Tours and in Paris at the shrine of St Geneviève. Shortly before
his death in 511 he presided over a national council at Orleans
which issued certain disciplinary rulings. In Burgundy, too, a
national council was held at Épaone (517), soon after the accession of the first Catholic king, presided over by Avitus of Vienne.
But in 534 Burgundy was annexed by the sons of Clovis, and in
536 the same fate befell the Ostrogothic kingdom of Provence.
With the exception of Septimania (under Visigothic rule) and
Brittany, Gaul was a nation once again under a Frankish empire
which extended also to parts of Germany.

This vast kingdom, sometimes divided up between contending
brothers and sometimes united under a stronger ruler such as
Clotair or Dagobert, was undoubtedly a Catholic country. But
compared with the flourishing Church of fifth-century Roman
Gaul and compared with the developments made in neighbouring
countries like Spain or England during the seventh century,
Frankish Catholicism seems debased and decadent. As in the
other Germanic countries, the monarchy controlled the episcopate, and it was the king who convoked national or regional
councils (there were five national councils between 511 and 614)
and made the appointments to vacant sees. But many sees were
left unfilled, while many of the appointments were unfortunate.
There were good bishops like St Nizier of Trier and Marovius of

Poitiers, the champions of the poor, or St Arnulf (or Arnoul) of Metz and others, but against such men there were episcopal brigands like Salonius of Embrun and Sagittarius of Gap, or simoniacs like Eusebius of Paris. The better examples were generally good administrators appointed by royal favour like Ouen of Rouen, Didier of Cahors and Eloi of Noyon (all officials of King Dagobert), and Léger of Autun, whose political activities ended perhaps unexpectedly in "martyrdom" under the palace mayor Ebroin in 678. The power of the metropolitans was negligible and their provincial jurisdiction completely disorganized in a country now ravaged by civil war and subjected to dynastic partitioning. The individual bishops hardly counted at all outside the towns where they resided, which were themselves gradually losing importance; there was a large increase in country parishes centred around village churches, but these were in the hands of local lords who did not greatly concern themselves with the religious life of the ignorant peasantry. Devoid of any intellectual or spiritual life, the Merovingian period was distinguished only by anarchy and decline.

In the literary field the only writer after St Caesarius of Arles, whose long episcopate (502–42) goes back beyond the Franks to the Visigoths and Ostrogoths and who is more noted for his activities and preaching than for his theology, is the historian Gregory of Tours (c. 540–94) whose uncritical work betrays an intellectual poverty. The accomplished poet Fortunatus, a monk who made his home at the convent of Queen Radegund in Poitiers, was an Italian exile who belonged in spirit to an earlier poetic tradition. After him writers, schools and sacred sciences were nowhere to be found.

The partial renewal of Christian life in the Frankish countries during the seventh century was again due to foreign influences. About 590 St Columba set out from Ireland on a journey which was to end in Luxeuil and northern Italy, and about 620 the Benedictine rule reached Southern Gaul and eventually Fleury-sur-Loire from Rome. These two new monastic movements, which soon merged, started a transformation of religious life in Gaul and the number of monasteries rapidly increased: a primitive observance was developed which was divided between agricultural work and the performance of the divine office. Monastic apostles like St Amand, St Vedast of Arras and St Omer of Thérouanne brought the Gospel back to the north and converted the Flemish pagans. Later, missionary monks from Anglo-Saxon England were to win over Germany, which became a part of Christendom under the Carolingian Empire.

PART III

CAROLINGIAN CHRISTIANITY

At this juncture, after three hundred years of division and dis-
memberment, Western Europe achieved unity once more under
a Frankish king of the House of Pepin, who in 800 retrieved and
claimed the ancient title of Emperor. In the eighth and ninth centuries the Carolingian State came to include nearly all the Latin
countries of the West, and Carolingian civilization extended even
beyond these frontiers to the Anglo-Saxon and Celtic lands. In
spite of the loss of Africa, Spain and the islands (Sicily, Sardinia,
Corsica and the Balearics) to Islam, Christendom found a champion in Charles Martel, who repulsed the Arabs at Poitiers in
732, and in Charlemagne, who wrested from the invader the Barcelona marches beyond the Pyrenees. These victories over the
infidels gave the Carolingian king an immense prestige and
established him as the acknowledged leader of Christendom.

CHAPTER IX

POPE AND EMPEROR

As in the Roman Empire and the Germanic kingdoms the part played by the sovereign in religious affairs was preponderant. What was unique in the Frankish monarchy was the sharing of this authority with the pope.

THE FRANKS ALLIED TO THE PAPACY

Gregory the Great, honoured and famed for his holiness, apostolic labours and missionary zeal, was followed by a quick succession of twenty-five popes between 604 and 731. The brevity of these pontificates (few of which lasted more than five years), the repressive Byzantine overlordship and troubles with the Lombards had prevented the papacy from exercising any effective authority in East or West. Moreover, the old conflict between the see of Rome and the Empire of Constantinople re-opened in the eighth century with the outbreak of the iconoclastic controversy, initiated by the emperor Leo III in 725. The imperial policy, condemned in 731 by Pope Gregory III, was continued after a short respite under the next emperor Constantine V, who not only revived (in 753 and 761) the harsh measures against the images or icons, but also forbade all forms of devotion to the saints as being idolatrous. Consequently Rome could no longer look to Byzantium for support in Italy, where the Lombards, in spite of their conversion to Catholicism, were seeking to become masters of the whole peninsula, including the various territories of the Roman Church known as the patrimony of St Peter. Gregory III and his successor Zacharias succeeded in coming to terms with the Lombard king Liutprand after many difficulties, but after the capture of Ravenna, the capital of the Byzantine exarchate, by King Astulf in 751, Zacharias resolved to appeal to the Franks.

Since the beginning of the eighth century the Frankish throne had been occupied by the last weak and decadent representative of the Merovingian dynasty, the *rois fainéants* (the "do nothing kings"), while the real power was in the hands of the "palace mayors": Pepin of Heristal, Charles Martel and Pepin the Short. In 747 Pepin the Short was left in sole command after removing the last Merovingian king and in 751, after consultation with Pope Zacharias and an assembly of the nobles, he had himself consecrated king, according to the rite of anointing hitherto followed in Visigothic Spain. In 754 the ceremony was repeated at Saint-Denis by the exiled Pope Stephen II, to whom Pepin offered refuge at the Frankish Court and from whom he obtained the title of Roman patrician in return for effective support against the Lombards. Two Frankish expeditions to Italy compelled Astulf to raise the siege of Rome and to yield to the pope all those central Italian territories from the mouth of the Tiber up to Ravenna and Bologna which now became the States of the Church. A lasting alliance had been welded between Rome and the Franks. The consecration of Pepin and the recognition of the Papal States marked for both the beginning of a new era: France now became "the Church's eldest daughter", and the papacy was mistress of a temporal power which remained almost unaltered right up to the nineteenth century.

CHARLEMAGNE AND THE CHURCH

With the acquisition of this political sovereignty, the independence of the Holy See seemed guaranteed. After 731 the Byzantine emperor was debarred from intervening in papal elections, whose procedure was reorganized in 769: the Roman clergy now became the sole electors, and their choice was restricted to one of the "cardinal" priests or deacons of Rome. But although the Byzantine overlordship had vanished and the

Lombards had ceased to be a threat after the destruction of their kingdom, the protection now offered by the Frankish monarchy was not without its inconveniences. Pepin's title of "patrician" was taken in 774 by his son Charles, who in 800 added to it the dignity of Emperor. This restoration of the Western Empire, marked by the solemn coronation of Charlemagne by Leo III in St Peter's, certainly reinforced the alliance established half a century earlier and widened the breach between the now predominantly Germanic West and the Byzantine East. But the Frankish monarch was now invested with a quasi-sacerdotal authority which made it all the easier for him to encroach on ecclesiastical affairs.

Examples of such encroachment are not hard to find, and indeed Charlemagne has been said to provide the link between the earlier Caesaropapism and the later Gallicanism. Not content with busying himself in the administration of the Papal States which he had reinforced and extended, he claimed the right of arbitrating doctrinal controversies, like the dispute over the Adoptianist heresy which had become widespread both in the Arab and Frankish dominions of Spain. According to the teaching proposed by Elipand, bishop of Toledo (and carried further by Felix of Urgel), Christ was simply a man, united to the Word to become the adoptive Son of God (hence the name Adoptianism). This heresy, which had already been formulated in the early centuries and bore a close resemblance to Nestorianism, was condemned at Frankfort in 794 by a council of bishops summoned from Gaul and Italy by Charlemagne. Papal condemnation followed in 798 and Felix of Urgel submitted in 800 after the Council of Aix-la-Chapelle.

The council of Frankfort also turned its attention to Iconoclasm, with a policy that ran counter to the mind of Rome. After the persecution by the emperor Constantine V, described above, the Iconoclastic troubles had come to an end with the accession of the empress Irene in 780, and seven years later the Catholic teaching on the veneration of images was formally defined by the seventh ecumenical council of Nicaea, which clearly distinguished between the concept of *latria*, worship reserved to God alone, and *dulia*, the reverence which could legitimately be paid to the saints or their images. But the acts of the council were so mistranslated in the Latin version which became current in the West that they were interpreted by Charlemagne and his circle as a defence of idolatry. Hence the appearance of the refutation known as the "Caroline Books", perhaps inspired by a desire to challenge the ecclesiastical claims of Constantinople. At any rate, the council of Frankfort went so far as to condemn the Nicaean decrees which had been ratified by the pope.

In another dispute which also related to the East, Charlemagne outdid the pope himself in punctilious concern for orthodoxy. A custom had been started (probably in Visigothic Spain *c.* 586) of adding to the Creed the statement that the Holy Spirit proceeds from the Father "and from the Son" (*Filioque*)—not "through the Son", as the Greeks said. Charlemagne's desire to humiliate Byzantine pride magnified this quibble over theological niceties out of all proportion, and each side accused the other of heterodoxy and innovation. Popes Hadrian and Leo III refused to treat the Greek formula as heretical, in spite of the categorical ruling of the Synod of Friuli in 796, and the *Filioque* was even omitted in the Latin and Greek texts of the Creed which Pope Leo had engraved in the Vatican basilica. But Charlemagne enforced his preferred version throughout his territories—a further source of conflict with the Byzantine patriarchate in the next century.

THE PAPACY IN THE NINTH CENTURY

Charlemagne lost no opportunity therefore of asserting himself as an arbiter in matters of faith. The docile or accommodating attitude of the papacy averted any violent clash between "the two halves of God", but in any case the supremacy of the "sacerdotal monarchy" did not long survive its originating genius. With the decline of the Empire under his successors, the Holy See once more gained the upper hand. At Aix-la-Chapelle in 811 the ageing Charlemagne had crowned his son Louis as emperor by his own hand, and Louis performed the same rite for his son Lothair in 817, but Pope Stephen IV insisted on repeating the coronation of Louis at Rheims in 816, and in 823 Paschal I did the same for Lothair at Rome. It was probably also this period which saw the appearance of the forgery known as the Donation of Constantine, which purported to record Constantine's relinquishment of all his Western territories to the pope. The document, though patently unauthentic, was accepted as genuine throughout the Middle Ages, and made it possible for the papacy to escape the obligations of gratitude which it had incurred by the recent donation of Pepin and to justify its claims to a sovereign authority in the West. In 833 Gregory IV came to Gaul to mediate between the emperor Louis the Pious and his rebellious sons, but his intervention only succeeded in dividing the bishops, in spite of support from Agobard of Lyons and others. In assembly with the Frankish nobles at Compiègne the bishops sentenced Louis to public penance and deposition, followed by absolution and reinstatement. And it was they again, during the civil wars which broke out between Louis' sons after his death in 840, who succeeded in preserving a moral unity between the three Carolingian kingdoms of France, Lotharingia and Germany.

This partition, settled at the treaty of Verdun (843), weakened the Empire and thereby allowed the papacy to assert its independence. The constitution of 824 which had made papal elections subject to imperial ratification was ignored at the accession of Leo IV in 847. In 850 the latter consecrated the emperor Louis of Italy, son of Lothair, whose attempt to set up an anti-pope to Benedict III in 855 met with no success. In the subsequent reign of Nicholas I (855–65) the papacy acquired a prestige unknown since the days of Gregory the Great. Unruly prelates like John of Ravenna and Hincmar of Rheims were resolutely brought to heel by this forceful pope, who disregarded imperial pleas in their favour. More impressive still was his uncompromising stand against the divorce of Lothair II, king of Lorraine, who had obtained the connivance of his court prelates. Pope and king were confronted in dramatic scenes at Rome, but neither Nicholas nor his successor Hadrian II yielded an inch. A fearless champion of the moral law, he never failed to assert the primacy of spiritual values, and, as a chronicler has it "he ruled kings and tyrants, subjecting them to his authority as if he had been sovereign of the world".

The Empire was now in full decline and it continued in name only because the pope still exercised his right of conferring the imperial crown on those members of the Carolingian dynasty who seemed capable of defending Italy against the Carolingian invaders. After the death of Lous II, the valiant adversary of the Mohammedan barbarians whom Adrian II had crowned a second time in 872, John VIII chose and consecrated Charles the Bald, youngest son of Louis the Pious, in 875, and then Charles the Fat in 881. But both princes proved ineffective, and the death of Charles the Fat in 888 marked the final close of the Empire. There were to be other emperors—like Guy of Spoleto, crowned by Stephen V in 891, Arnulf of Germany by Formosus in 896, Guy's son Lambert by John IX in 898, Louis of Provence by Benedict IV in 901, Berengar of Friuli by John X in 915—but their coronations were without significance or result, and they themselves obtained neither power nor prestige from an illusory dignity.

Yet the papacy gained as little from the disappearance of the Carolingian Empire as did the kingdoms carved out of its old territory. While the latter were overwhelmed by a new succession of barbarian invaders (Saracens, Normans, Avars and Hungarians) and torn apart by a prevailing feudal anarchy, the popes became the tools of the Roman aristocracy, and the shameful outrage inflicted on the body of Pope Formosus in 897 symbolizes the degradation to which the Holy See had sunk. The fall of the Empire seemed to envelop the papacy to which it had been bound so closely for a century and a half.

CHAPTER X

THE ECCLESIASTICAL
RESTORATION

The Church had gained certain compensating advantages from the intervention of the State in her affairs. It was the Carolingians who were responsible for restoring the institutional structure of the Church, which had been in complete decay since the seventh century.

THE POSSESSIONS OF THE CHURCH

The restoration of governmental authority by the founder of the Carolingian dynasty, Charles Martel, had been marked by an appropriation of ecclesiastical possessions and titles: episcopal and parochial property was handed over to the Frankish warriors, and those sees which were not left vacant fell into the hands of laymen or unworthy clerics. This process of secularization was the cause of a general decline in the observance and morals of the clergy. Under Carloman and Pepin, the sons of Charles Martel, who became aware of these abuses, the necessary reforms were taken into active consideration and a certain amount of property was restored (for example, to the abbey of Saint-Denis), but the process was slow and piecemeal and the actual measures subsequently taken during the course of the eighth century often led only to new and more systematic spoliations. Church property was now "let" to tenants who paid a quit-rent and were bound to see to the upkeep or restoration of the requisitioned church. The capitularies of Pepin and Charlemagne also revived and enforced the practice whereby every farmer paid the parish a "tithe" of his agricultural produce.

REFORM OF THE CLERGY

More important, however, than this restoration of the Church's material goods was the movement of religious reform, first undertaken in the reign of Pepin by the English missionary Boniface who had become a bishop in Germany. While inheriting the tradition of the Irish monks who had come to Gaul in the preceding century he exercised an influence that was more profound and less anarchic, thanks to the combined support of the pope and the palace mayor. As papal legate he presided over a series of councils in Austrasia and Neustria between 742 and 747, at which momentous decrees were promulgated: priests and bishops were bound to the obligations of celibacy, fixed residence, and a worthy and edifying way of life; severe penalties were laid down for offenders and for vagrant monks or clerics; examinations were instituted for ordinands and, at the time of an episcopal visitation or diocesan synod, for parish priests, while bans were laid on superstitious customs and on marriage within the degrees of affinity. Preventive measures were taken against a resurgence of anarchy by reinstituting regular councils and by restoring the authority of the metropolitans. In Neustria Boniface re-established the metropolitan sees of Rouen, Rheims and Sens, while in Austrasia he himself took the position of sole primate (like the Archbishop of Canterbury in England) with his see at Mainz. The national council of 747 finally drafted a declaration of loyalty to the Holy See, including a request that the pallium should be sent to every metropolitan.

Many of these decrees fell into disuse after the death of Boniface, and it was left to Charlemagne to complete and carry into effect the work of reform in his capitularies and in the councils summoned on his initiative. The metropolitan sees of the Empire were at last re-established and their holders, now called archbishops, had certain suffragans under their jurisdiction, while above them were the arch-chaplain of the Court and the legates appointed by the king to superintend the activities of the bishops. The king reserved the right of appointing all the bishops himself. Provision was also made for priests, who were now required to possess a minimum amount of knowledge and the ability to preach to the faithful (in the vernacular, not Latin), while those living in towns were bound to community life for the better observance of their moral and spiritual obligations: the conventual rule of Chrodegang of Metz was widely adopted in Austrasia and a similar rule for the whole Empire was issued by the council of Aix-la-Chapelle in 817. Lastly, every see was now to have its chapter of canons.

This *Ordo canonicus* for the secular clergy was accompanied by a corresponding *Ordo regularis* for the monks. Here, with his constant concern for regulation and uniformity, Charlemagne enforced the universal observance of the Benedictine rule, and his capitulary of 817 provided both the main lines and the details of reform. The instrument of this policy was the Septimanian nobleman Witiza, better known as Benedict of Aniane (750–821). This monk of austere life was entrusted by Louis the Pious with the task of reorganizing the monasteries of Aquitaine and later with the foundation of a model abbey near Aix-la-Chapelle where all the future monastic superiors of Europe were to receive their formation.

THE LITURGY

It was also due to royal intervention that the liturgy took on its final shape and definitive formulation. The liturgy at Rome had been almost entirely the work of Gregory the Great, who had simplified the earlier Leonine and Gelasian sacramentaries, but the countries north of the Alps had seen the independent development of the Gallican and Mozarabic liturgies. Under Pepin the use of the Gelasian sacramentary and the Roman method of liturgical chant were widely encouraged, and subsequently Charlemagne obtained from Pope Hadrian the Gregorian Sacramentary which he completed by excerpts from the Gelasian: henceforward this was the Missal in general use throughout the Empire. The reform affected not only the ordinary of the Mass and the monastic Office, but also the selection of Epistles and Gospels, the text of liturgical hymns and even the arrangement of the seasonal and sanctoral calendar. The palatine chapel at Aix served as a practical school of liturgy and did much to unify varieties of worship according to the Roman pattern.

Religious life, then, was centred on the liturgy, and indeed the whole age, with its concern for the Carolingian values of order, form and regularity, has been characterized as a "liturgical culture". But the tendency was towards a rather stiff ritualism which neglected instinctive spontaneity and was unsympathetic to personal piety. The common prayers were said in Latin, a language now becoming the preserve of scholars, unintelligible to the people, and were in part recited inaudibly; private Masses began to appear alongside the common Office, causing an increase in the number of altars in the church; at Mass the celebrant no longer faced the people, ordinary bread was not used, and the practice of frequent communion which had lapsed in earlier times does not seem to have been restored. To all intents and purposes the faithful had become merely spectators at the sacrifice. Moral and spiritual life, too, seems to have been restricted to a routine conformity, and documents like the manual of Dhuoda, a ninth century princess, give us a glimpse of a rather joyless and dry religion. The casuistical system of the Irish penitentials was abandoned and an attempt made to reinforce public penance for public sins.

LAW AND LEGEND

This age of order also saw the formation of Canon Law. The canons of earlier councils were assembled by learned clerics into authoritative collections like the great *Dionyso-Hadriana*, drawn up at Rome and current in Gaul by 774, or the Spanish compilation known as the *Hispana*. Some of the compilers did not scruple to supplement the genuine documents with a variety of complete forgeries such as the spurious capitularies of pseudo-Benedict and the false decretals attributed to early popes by a self-styled "Isidore". The purpose of these Isidorian documents, which probably originated near Le Mans about 850 and soon gained a wide circulation in Western Europe, was to surround the contemporary reforming movement with an aura of antiquity.

This veneration felt by the Church of Gaul for tradition may also explain the number of legends which now sprang up in its midst. Episcopal registers which seemed too short were brought up to strength with imaginary names which enabled the evangelization of the mission and the foundation of many of its bishoprics to be traced back to apostolic origins. The story of St Mary Magdalen and the holy women of Provence has remained the most famous of these legends, but we may also note the location of the tomb of the apostle St James at Compostela in Spain, and the identification of St Denys, the third century martyr and first bishop of Paris, with Dionysius the Areopagite, known in the East as the author of a number of mystical treatises.

CHAPTER XI

THE INTELLECTUAL
RENAISSANCE

Carolingian literature was not restricted however to the compilation of canons or the formulation of liturgical texts. There was
also a great deal of original work—part of that general advance
of culture which we known as the Carolingian Renaissance. Here
again the impetus came from Charlemagne himself. It was he who
ordered the setting up of elementary schools in every diocese and
monastery "for the teaching of the psalms, singing and grammar" (according to his capitulary of 789). At the court he
founded the Palatine Academy, soon renowned for its neo-
Roman ideals and for the correct and classical Latin spoken
there, and he acted as patron to foreign scholars who came to
direct this intellectual work he valued so highly.

SACRED LITERATURE

From Italy he brought Peter of Pisa, grammarian and occasional poet, Paul the Deacon, another grammarian and versifier
and Paulinus of Aquileia, a third grammarian turned theologian.
More lasting than these Italians, whose stay at the court was but
brief, were other foreigners such as Theodulf, the Spaniard whom
Charlemagne made bishop of Orleans, a versatile poet and a man
of remarkable zeal who even turned his hand to theology with
his treatise on the Holy Spirit, written to support Charlemagne's
position in the *Filioque* controversy. Most famous of all these
writers was the Englishman Alcuin (730–804), the master of the

School of York, whom Charlemagne originally met in Italy. After many years of service he became abbot of the monastery of St Martin of Tours, which he ruled till his death. His influence over the period was considerable, especially in the field of education where ¹ ɛ organized the teaching of the system of the "liberal arts" whic. had been inherited from the late Empire. He also composed some minor poetry and sound works of theology and exegesis.

Other monasteries, which were destined to have a far-reaching influence under Louis the Pious, became centres of intellectual activity during these years. In the monastic scriptoria countless works of classical antiquity, both sacred and profane, were copied out in the beautiful characteristic "Carolingian" script, and some of the great abbots themselves composed encyclopedic treatises. East of the Rhine was the abbey of Fulda, home of Rhabanus Maurus who died as Archbishop of Mainz in 856, and Reichenau, ruled from 808 to 849 by Walafrid Strabo: both these men were not only exegetes but hagiographers, canonists and liturgists as well. Then there was Liège, home of the Irishman Sedulius; Prum, with its poet Wandalbert; Weissenburg had the exegete Otfrid; Saint-Denis had Hilduin; at Ferrières was Lupus, the disciple of Rhabanus Maurus, who corresponded with the great men of his day; at St Wandrille, Gervold and Ansegise; at St Riquier, Angilbert; at Corbie, Paschasius Radbertus and Ratramnus. Aix-la-Chapelle produced Eginhard, Charlemagne's biographer, and later came John Scotus Erigena, an Irish exile at the court of Charles the Bald, who translated from the Greek the treatises of Dionysius the Areopagite and the works of Gregory of Nazianzus and Gregory of Nyssa, besides composing a philosophical work on nature and creation.

Outside the abbeys there were bishops too who distinguished themselves in the fields of intellectual and pastoral activity. Agobard of Lyons was a polemical writer whose broadsides were delivered at heretics, Jews and officialdom, while his rival Amalarius and the archdeacon Florus both wrote commentaries on the Mass according to their different methods. Other names were

Jonas of Orleans, a writer on monarchy, and Hincmar, the proud and forceful metropolitan of Rheims.

HERESIES

The occasional heresies which not unnaturally emerged from this feverish literary activity were opposed with fiery intensity: the theological controversies of the period reveal its intellectual vitality. About 840 the dispute about free will which had been in abeyance since the Council of Orange in 529 was reopened by the priest Gottschalk, whose exaggeration of the Augustinian teaching on predestination led to his condemnation by Rhabanus Maurus (848) and imprisonment in a monastery of the diocese of Soissons. When Hincmar of Rheims summoned a council to condemn him at Quiercy (849), the defenders of the Augustinian tradition rallied to the support of Gottschalk and among those who took their stand on predestination were Ratramnus, Bishop Prudentius of Troyes, Florus and Remi of Lyons, and above all Lupus of Ferrières. The battle lasted for several more years, intensified by the passion of Gottschalk and the high-handed procedure of Hincmar, who aroused enmity at Lyons and Rome alike. The council of Soissons (853) was challenged by that of Valence (855): eventually a compromise formula was promulgated in 860 at the council of Thuzey (Lorraine), but Gottschalk refused to abjure his errors and remained under condemnation.

Another unresolved controversy was occasioned by a treatise on the Eucharist written *c.* 840 by the abbot of Corbie, Paschasius Radbertus. Rhabanus Maurus, Ratramnus and Gottschalk attacked the work for its excessively "material" view of the real presence. Radbertus slightly modified his position in his reply (*c.* 855) and there the matter remained.

RELIGIOUS ART

The artistic renaissance accompanying the intellectual renaissance under Charlemagne was marked by the same characteristics, a return to antiquity and a sense of splendour, which were now put at the service of the established religion. Building materials still remained much the same: fully-dressed stone construction was exceptional and wood was always used extensively, especially for church roofs. But there was a return to old forms such as the basilica, octagon or rotunda, and sometimes ancient materials were used for the construction of important buildings: the imperial chapel at Aix was built of stones from the ramparts of Verdun and of marble and pillars from a Ravenna palace. This chapel—in the shape of an octagon crowned by a cupola—was a large scale version of San Vitale (each side measuring nearly thirty-three yards) and it served as a model for many other churches. In some places there were certain innovations. At Cologne and elsewhere there were two apses facing each other on either side of the central nave, and in other churches (at St Riquier, for example) there was a belfry or lantern-tower above the transept. The few surviving specimens of Carolingian architecture today are mostly in the form of vaulted crypts, like those of Saint-Médard at Soissons, Saint-Quentin, Senlis, etc.

A more familiar characteristic of the period is its decorative art, in which a figurative style succeeded the earlier barbarian linear designs. There are few carved capitals and sarcophagi but the lack of stone sculpture, which is confined to some crudely embellished paving, is amply compensated in other art-forms: mural mosaics, as at Germigny-les-Prés, stucco bas-reliefs, as at Santa-Maria-in-Valle in Friuli, and altar plaques of chased metal. Best of all were individual architectural features or objets d'art: statuettes, like the bronze Charlemagne in Metz Cathedral; wooden statue-reliquaries cased in gold or silver, like the famous Sainte-Foy at Conques; caskets or bindings of ivory carved with human figures—contrasting with the simpler Anglo-Saxon caskets of chased whalebone; illuminated manuscripts, Gospel-books or Sacramentaries, with frontispiece portraits, decorated initials and varied colouring; figured embroidery on linen or silk material, in the Byzantine style. All these minor arts show a return to naturalism, competing with ornamental, geometric or floral motifs typical of the earlier Germanic or Celtic styles.

CHAPTER XII

THE EXPANSION OF THE CHURCH

Under the aspects considered above, Carolingian Christianity has been studied chiefly in terms of its return to the past. But the period was also one of progress and advance after the barbarian crisis, and the territory of the Western Church at last burst the boundaries of the former Roman Empire. Already by the end of the Merovingian period Irish and Anglo-Saxon monk-missionaries had penetrated beyond the Rhine, and this pioneering activity now reached its climax in the eighth century with the mission of St Boniface, the apostle of Germany.

ST BONIFACE

The first missionary to reach Frisia had been Wilfrid of York, in the course of his travels between England and Rome, soon after 678. Shortly afterwards abbot Egbert sent out Witbert, followed by twelve more monks under the leadership of the Northumbrian Willibrord (657–739) who received episcopal consecration, with the new name of Clement, from Pope Sergius I and became the first bishop of Utrecht, under the protection of Pepin of Héristal and Charles Martel. About the same time an Irish missionary, Fridolin, was preaching in Southern Germany, while Reichenau on Lake Constance and several other monasteries in Alsace were founded by the monk Pirmin. More monasteries were founded by Rupert of Worms in the region of Salzburg and by the Irishman Kilian in Thuringia. Emmeran of

Poitiers, after preaching at Ratisbon, had met a martyr's death at Salzburg.

Most important of all these missionaries was the Anglo-Saxon monk Wilfrid, who enlisted the joint support of the Frankish king and the papacy. In 719 at the age of forty-five he received the Roman name of Boniface from Gregory IV together with detailed instructions for an official mission to Germany. For ten years he based himself on Hesse and Thuringia, where his labours bore fruit in countless conversions, thanks to the missionary policy prompted by Daniel of Winchester (drawing his inspiration from Gregory the Great) and thanks to the devoted English monks and nuns who joined him. In 732, ten years after his episcopal consecration at Rome, he was nominated archbishop, with the task of setting up a hierarchy in the regions of the Weser, Main and Danube. He began in Bavaria (formerly Roman territory) by restoring the bishoprics of Salzburg, Freising, Passau and Ratisbon, while further north he established new bishoprics at Buraburg, Erfurt, Wurzburg and Eichstadt. His monastic foundations extended throughout the country: Fritzlar, Amoeneburg, Ohrdruff and above all Fulda (744), soon a great abbey of four hundred monks, directly dependent on the Holy See. We have seen already the work which this heroic missionary undertook for the reorganization of the Frankish church in Gaul: later he returned to Mainz as bishop and permanent legate of the pope, primate of those Rhineland territories which were now as firmly joined to Christendom as they had already been to the Frankish Empire. Eventually in 754, in a still pagan district of Frisia, he met the glorious death of a martyr.

CHARLEMAGNE AND THE SAXONS

The conversion of Saxony (between the Rhine and the Elbe) undertaken at the end of the eighth century did not follow the essentially religious lines of Boniface's mission. It was not a question of stamping out pagan survivals in some corner of imperial territory, for Saxony lay outside the frontiers of Christendom and the Empire. Disregarding the directives of Rome, which were opposed to any kind of constraint, Charlemagne resolved to accomplish conversion and conquest simultaneously. After his first victorious expedition in 776 the defeated Saxon warriors were baptized in a body; the subsequent revolt of Widekind, accompanied by a general apostasy, was followed by terrible repressions in 784 and 793. The death penalty was decreed not only for the killing of a cleric but for refusal to undergo baptism and even for failure to observe the Lenten fast, while the new vassals were forced to pay very heavy tithes and resistance was in many cases punished by deportation. This reign of terror only succeeded in exciting hatred for Christianity, and Alcuin protested indignantly against a violence so alien to the spirit of the Gospel. Yet the new religion survived its shameful beginnings and soon became firmly entrenched, so that a hierarchy was established even within Charlemagne's lifetime. Willenad, one of the missionaries of Frisia, was consecrated as bishop of Bremen in 787, and two other bishoprics were established at Verden and Minden in the valley of the Weser. Under Louis the Pious more sees were set up at Hamburg, Hildesheim and Halberstadt in Eastphalia, and in Westphalia at Munster, Osnabruck and Paderborn, while Corvey on the Weser (founded in 822 from Corbie in Picardy) was the first of many monasteries which fostered an authentic Christian way of life.

To the south-east of the Carolingian Empire the Gospel was brought to the Slovenes of Carinthia by Arn, later archbishop of Salzburg, and Paulinus of Aquileia, who both followed the advice of Alcuin in adopting gentler methods.

BEYOND THE IMPERIAL FRONTIER

On the initiative of the pope and the emperor—always working in concert—some missions were undertaken outside the orbit of Frankish rule. In 823 Denmark was penetrated by Ebbo of Rheims and Halitgar of Cambrai, and the Danish king Harald received baptism. The country was then evangelized by a monk of Corvey, Anscar, who later crossed to Sweden and in 831 became the first bishop of Hamburg and papal legate for the whole of Scandinavia. But these early results were soon seen to be transitory: a violent pagan reaction broke out in Sweden and had already spread to Hamburg when that town was destroyed by Norman pirates in 845. Anscar fell back on Bremen and renewed his efforts with undaunted energy, sending out fresh missionaries to Sweden and Denmark, but his death in 865 marked the end of this first phase of Christianity and two more centuries were to pass before the final conversion of Scandinavia.

The conversion of the Slav lands had been accomplished at an earlier date by missionaries from the Eastern Church. It may have been from Germany that Christianity reached Moravia in the reign of Rastilav, before 850, but it was to Byzantium that the newly converted king turned for missionary bishops. In answer to his appeal the Greek brothers Constantine (known as Cyril) and Methodius arrived to spread the Gospel in 862. With the approval of the pope and the patriarch of Constantinople they used the Slav language for the liturgy.

There were no missions in the countries to the north-west of the Carolingian Empire: the flourishing state of Christianity in the Anglo-Saxon and Irish kingdoms has been described above. Nevertheless Charlemagne intervened in English affairs to the extent of arbitrating political disputes involving the bishops. In the ninth century the island Churches were threatened by the heathen Viking invaders from Scandinavia, but Celtic and Saxon resistance did not exclude efforts to convert the enemy. Under "the English Charlemagne", Alfred of Wessex (871–899), lawgiver and patron of letters, the Danish chieftain Guthorm received baptism, and his example was followed by Rollo when in 910 he settled in continental "Normandy".

Lastly the lands to the south-west, beyond the Pyrenees, had been converted long before the arrival of Charlemagne: the march of Barcelona which he wrested from the Arabs was an ancient centre of Christianity and so too was the kingdom of Leon, northern stronghold of Iberian independence, where the shrine of St James at Compostela was already beginning to draw pilgrims. Here the Franks came not as missionaries but as crusaders against the infidel.

As the leader of Latin Christendom, Charlemagne also turned his attention to the fate of those Churches which had fallen under the yoke of Islam. After several diplomatic exchanges the caliph of Baghdad, Harun al Rashid, agreed to recognize a kind of Frankish protectorate in the Holy Places, and the patriarch of Jerusalem accompanied the gift of relics to the royal chapel at Aix with an appeal for support for the oppressed Churches. Large sums in alms were collected and dispatched by the Frankish kings and in addition Western pilgrims, tolerated by the Muslim authorities, kept alive the devotion to Christ's tomb.

In the ninth century, therefore, the prestige and influence of the Frankish emperor prevailed throughout Christendom, not only within his imperial frontiers from Rome to Aix and from Barcelona to Hamburg, but even at York, Jerusalem and Constantinople. The Byzantine emperors Nicephorus I and Michael I both corresponded with Charlemagne on equal terms, in spite of his being an "usurper" of the imperial title, and in 824 these good relations were reinforced by the embassies which finally led to the settlement of the iconoclastic dispute: after the restoration of orthodoxy following the council of Paris in 825 and the council of Constantinople in 843 emperors, pope and patriarch found themselves in complete accord. But this perfect balance was not long maintained, for the end of the century saw the slow but sure decline of the Carolingian Empire.

THE DARK AGES

The Christian world at the turn of the eighth and ninth centuries fell into three distinct domains, each separated from the other by different obstacles: the territories subject to Islam in the South, the Byzantine empire in the East, and the former Carolingian empire in the West.

THE MUSLIM COUNTRIES

In the Arab empire which stretched from Spain to Persia by way of the Maghreb, Egypt and Syria, Christianity had suffered a decline which amounted to almost total annihilation, and if there were scattered survivals we do not know precisely what forms they took. Though there was no direct persecution, numbers gradually began to fall away under the pressure of self-interest or environment and eventually most of the bishoprics and monasteries disappeared. Organized Christian life continued only in Spain: more flexible than the Eastern Abbassids, the Ommiads of Cordova were perhaps frightened into a policy of toleration by the successes of the threatening Christian reconquista. In the other Arab lands Christian life was almost entirely extinguished, and the later history of these shadow Churches is lost in obscurity.

THE GREEK LANDS OF THE EAST

The Byzantine Church on the other hand steadily continued the traditions of the Late Empire, and in many respects attained during this period its highest culmination. With the end of the iconoclastic controversy in 843 and the accession of the Macedonian dynasty in 867 Church and Empire alike took on a new lease of life and vigour. Under the Patriarch Photius and the Emperor Constantine Porphyrogenitus literature and the arts, deeply imbued with a religious spirit, flourished with unsurpassed splendour: cupola-crowned basilicas, mosaics and illumination, encyclopedias and theological treatises, are all expressions of a brilliant revival. Under Byzantine influence also the Christian faith and hierarchical order was extended into the very heart of continental Europe, with the conversion of the Czechs, the Bulgars and later the Russians. Yet now that the West was in decline, even these successes only stiffened Eastern arrogance. Just as Innocent I had supported Chrysostom in 404, so Pope Nicholas I refused to recognize the deposition of the Patriarch Ignatius in 859, treating his successor Photius as a usurper and a miscreant. Fuel was added to the flames by the sending of papal legates to Bulgaria in answer to a Bulgar appeal, and the conflict ended in a schism lasting from 863 to 867. Unity was eventually restored with the departure of the leading protagonists and after a further series of fluctuations: in 879 Pope John VIII had recognized Photius and accepted the Byzantine version of the *Credo*. But the headstrong patriarch was finally deposed by a new emperor and henceforward the appointment of the head of the Greek Church became an imperial prerogative. Thus, in effect, since the other Oriental patriarchs were robbed of all real influence under Muslim rule, the emperor tended to become the exclusive head of the Eastern Church, and the authority of Rome—hitherto recognized at least in principle—was often ignored or disregarded.

THE LATIN WEST

The Holy See itself had fallen at this very time into deplorable decay which robbed it of all prestige and weight. The passing of the Carolingian Empire had left Rome in the hands of the lords of the Campagna, notably the family of Theophylact, whose wife Theodora and daughter Marozia virtually reigned over the

Roman Church between 904 and 935, using Sergius III, John X and John XI as the instruments of their ambitious designs. The next four popes, all eliminated in quick succession, were followed by the degenerate John XII (955–63), and the record of the papacy now became one of tragedy and crime, murder and debauchery "which soiled the papal throne with blood and filth".

Just as the darkness was enveloping Rome, anarchy was spreading throughout the West. The Carolingian kingdoms were split up among countless petty nobles and everywhere the Church fell into the hands of powerful laymen, who appropriated bishoprics, parishes and monasteries which they sacrificed to their own material interests. Simony (trafficking in the orders or sacraments of the Church) and Nicolaitism (clerical marriage or concubinage) prevailed everywhere, and the Church, pervaded with worldliness, seemed incapable of reforming or purifying the corrupt, brutal and superstitious society. How long could Western Christendom survive, rotten as it was with internal decay?

Yet this gloom and chaos was relieved by glimmerings of light which promised better things to come. Cluny, founded in 910, was one of several monasteries which maintained the true Christian way of life in the midst of the tenth century, and several Christian kings worked vigorously for reform: Otto the Great who restored the Empire under his own sovereignty in 962 installed a more worthy episcopate in his German territories. And if the intrusions of Otto and his successors at Rome were in principle reprehensible they effectively put an end to the rule of "pornocracy". The reform of the Church had been started, and at the turn of the millenium (c. 1000 A.D.) the era of medieval Christendom was in sight.

SELECT BIBLIOGRAPHY

In this series: CANU, Jean: *The Religious Orders of Men*; CRISTIANI, Léon: *Heresies and Heretics*; d'ORMESSON, Wladimir: *The Papacy*.

BEDE, Venerable: *History of the English Church and People*, translated by J. Sherley-Price, London and Baltimore, Penguin Books, 1953.

BETTENSEN, H.: *Documents of the Christian Church*, London and New York, Oxford Univ. Press, 1943.

BUTLER, Cuthbert: *Benedictine Monachism*, London and New York, Longmans, 1924.

Cambridge Medieval History, volumes 1–4; *Shorter Cambridge Medieval History*, volume I, Cambridge and New York, 1952.

DEANESLY, Margaret: *History of Europe, 476–911*, London, Methuen and New York, Barnes and Noble, 1956; *History of the Medieval Church, 590–1500*, London, Methuen and Nashville, Tenn., British Book Centre, 1954.

DUCKETT, E. S.: *Latin Writers of the Fifth Century*, New York, Henry Holt, 1930.

DUDDEN, F. H.: *Life and Times of St Ambrose*, London and New York, Oxford Univ. Press, 1935.

FREND, W. H. C.: *The Donatist Church*, London and New York, Oxford Univ. Press, 1952.

HOARE, F. R.: *The Western Fathers*, London and New York, Sheed and Ward, 1954.

HUGHES, Philip: *A History of the Church*, three volumes, London and New York, Sheed and Ward, 1934–47; *A Popular History of the Catholic Church*, London, Burns Oates and New York, Macmillan, 1939.

JALLAND, Trevor: *Life and Times of St Leo the Great*, London, S.P.C.K. and New York, Macmillan, 1940.

LOT, Ferdinand: *The End of the Ancient World*, New York, Barnes and Noble, 1953.

MEER, F. van der, and MOHRMANN, Christine: *Atlas of the Early Christian World*, London and New York, Nelson, 1958.

O'MEARA, J. J.: *The Young Augustine*, London and New York, Longmans, 1954.

PALANQUE, J. R. (Editor): *The Church in the Christian Roman Empire*, two volumes, London, Burns Oates and New York, Macmillan, 1949.

POURRAT, Pierre: *Christian Spirituality*, volumes I and II, London, Burns Oates, 1922–3, and Westminster, Md, Newman Press, 1953–6.

PRESTIGE, G. L.: *Fathers and Heretics*, London, S.P.C.K. and New York, Macmillan, 1940.

WALBANK, F. W.: *Decline of the Roman Empire in the West*, New York, Abelard Schumann, 1953.

The Twentieth Century Encyclopedia of Catholicism

The number of each volume indicates its place in the over-all series and not the order of publication.

TWENTIETH CENTURY ENCYCLOPEDIA OF CATHOLICISM

All titles are subject to change.